KAYCAN
Proudly supports

THE KILEE PATCHELL-EVANS
AUTISM RESEARCH GROUP

SUPPORTING THE COMMUNITY
AND BUILDING
LASTING IMPRESSIONS.

www.kaycan.com

COOKING WITH CANADA'S BEST

SIGNATURE RECIPES FROM OUR FINEST CHEFS

Project and book created by Karen Dubrofsky Publications

Photographs by Fahri Yavuz

Sponsored by

GoodLife
FITNESS

A Bastian Book

ECW PRESS
ecwpress.com

All proceeds from the sale of this book will be donated to
the Kilee Patchell-Evans Autism Research Group.

Author and Editor-in-Chief
Karen Dubrofsky

Photographs by Fahri Yavuz, www.yavuzphoto.ca

Graphic Design
Julie Siciliano and Martine Chartier, Cassi Design
www.cassidesign.com

Recipes edited by Jane Pavanel, Knockout Communications

Food Testers
Karen Dubrofsky, Lori Raiken, Anna Maria Ponzi

Nutritional Analysis
Leonard A. Piche PhD RD, Kimberly L. Zammit, Meredith M. McQuade

Sponsorship
Megan Cameron, GoodLife Fitness Clubs

Advertising
Natalie Spoozak

Legal Consultant
David Himelfarb

Official Travel Sponsors
Air Canada Kids' Horizons and Fairmont Hotels

Printed in Canada by Transcontinental

Copyright © Karen Dubrofsky, 2009

A Bastian Book, published by ECW Press, 2120 Queen Street East, Suite 200,
Toronto, Ontario, Canada M4E 1E2 / 416.694.3348 / info@ecwpress.com

ISBN 978-1-55022-912-7

Cataloguing in Publication Data available from Library and Archives Canada.

This book is printed on Influence Softgloss 160m paper.

A NOTE TO COOKS: COOKING WITH CANADA'S BEST is a labour of love, created through a collaboration
between Canada's finest chefs and our dedicated volunteers. Although every effort was made to ensure an
accurate translation from the chefs' imaginations to these pages, we hope you will forgive any omissions
or errors. Also note that the photographs are included for inspiration and reference, and may differ in
presentation from the recipes as written.

Two recipes from *One Pot Italian Cooking: More Than 100 Easy Authentic Recipes* were reproduced here:
Lamb Ribs and Classic Zabaglioni. Copyright © 2007. Reproduced with the permission of Massimo Capra
and Madison Press Books.

www.cookingwithcanadasbest.com

On behalf of the Kilee Patchell-Evans Autism Research Group, thank you for purchasing *Cooking with Canada's Best* and supporting groundbreaking autism research.

Today one in every 150 children in Canada is diagnosed with autism. As a parent I can tell you that autistic children often exist in a world of isolation, unable to relate to the people around them and enjoy the routines we all take for granted for our children. Going to school, playing with friends, telling their parents they love them are challenges faced every day by autistic children and their families.

But there is hope! The Kilee Patchell-Evans Autism Research Group, named after my thirteen-year-old daughter Kilee, has unfolded some important new findings that are receiving global attention. Dr. Derrick MacFabe, the director of the group, has a remarkable research team located at the University of Western Ontario. This research was recognized by the Canadian Medical Association in 2007 with its Medal of Honour. Together, Dr. MacFabe and I will continue to build collaborations between scientists and concerned citizens around the world.

The Kilee Patchell-Evans Autism Research Group is grateful to Karen Dubrofsky for her generosity in donating the proceeds from this amazing cookbook to help us find the cause and the cure for autism.

Once again, thank you for your support, and enjoy these signature recipes from Canada's finest chefs!

For more information visit:
www.psychology.uwo.ca/autism.htm

David Patchell-Evans
Founder & CEO GoodLife Fitness

Cooking with Canada's Best brings together signature recipes from some of the most talented and renowned chefs in Canada, all for the sake of raising money for autism research. The recipes are easy to follow, so almost everyone can make these delicious meals at home.

Creating this book was an unforgettable experience. It gave me the opportunity to travel across Canada, from the shores of Newfoundland to the coast of British Columbia, and experience the beauty of this country and the generous hospitality of its people.

During the initial stages of putting the book together I was uncertain how it would be received. As a volunteer who has never fundraised as a professional, I was concerned that with people already committed to so many important charitable causes, would I garner enough interest to support research into autism? To my surprise, within five minutes of emailing my first chef, I received a phone call from him confirming that he would love to participate in the book and its worthy cause. From that moment, I felt confident that it would succeed in its purpose.

As the months passed and I worked on this project and learned more about autism, I was overwhelmed by the vast number of people affected by it. As I approached companies, restaurants and individuals to contribute to the book, I was struck by the strong presence of autism across our country. I recall one of the contributing chefs telling me that "a project like this needs to be done." He revealed that his best friend's child is autistic, and that he understood firsthand the need for more research.

The idea of linking this book to autism research was encouraged by David Patchell-Evans, a philanthropist with an inspiring vision. Within moments of conversing with him, I could feel his passion to help find a cure and realized how urgently funds were needed. I thank Patch for all of his support.

I would like to express my deepest appreciation to the chefs appearing in *Cooking with Canada's Best* for so generously allowing me into their kitchens. I am most grateful for the opportunity they gave me to witness their cooking in action and to sample all the healthful and delectable recipes they shared along the way. They are all artists in the true sense of the word. Their love for their work shines through in their gastronomic creations.

So, please enjoy cooking alongside these great chefs as you make the recipes inside this book, and know that by purchasing *Cooking with Canada's Best*, you have contributed to finding a cure for autism.

This cookbook would not have been possible without the participation of some wonderful people. To Megan Cameron, Natalie Spoozak, Julie Siciliano and Flano Castelli, I say thank you; and to Fahri Yavuz, I'd like to express my sincere appreciation for tirelessly travelling the country with me and shooting such outstanding photos.

As you can imagine, a project of this magnitude required considerable time away from family. A special thank you to my husband Lionel and children Andrew, Lisa and Philip, for your support and encouragement.

I also dedicate this book to a dear friend who passed away before this project began, a man who encouraged me tremendously to start working on it. Michael Bick, you are not forgotten.

Karen Korzinstone Dubrofsky
Author and editor-in-chief

www.cookingwithcanadasbest@gmail.com

author
editor-in-chief

Appetizers

Shrimp with Fennel and Apple Salad

8 13-15 black tiger shrimp
Salt and freshly ground pepper
Fennel and apple salad
Herb mousse
Citrus vinaigrette
Plate decoration: coriander tuile,
red pepper oil

CITRUS VINAIGRETTE:
2 oranges, juiced
2 lemons, juiced
4 limes, juiced
1 tbsp (15 ml) wasabi paste
1 cup (250 ml) grape seed oil
2 tbsp (30 ml) mirin

FENNEL AND APPLE SALAD:
1 fennel bulb, cut in half
2 Macintosh apples, cored, peel on
2 tbsp (30 ml) extra-virgin olive oil
Juice of ½ lemon
Juice of ½ lime

HERB MOUSSE:
1 bunch coriander
1 bunch tarragon
2 stuffed cups (500 ml) baby spinach
2 tsp (10 ml) minced garlic
6 tbsp (90 ml) water
6 tbsp (90 ml) extra-virgin olive oil

CORIANDER TUILE (optional):
1 cup (250 ml) egg whites
7 oz (200 g) sugar
¾ tsp (3½ ml) salt
7 oz (200 g) flour
9 oz (250 g) butter, melted and clarified
1½ tsp (7 ml) ground coriander
¼ tsp (1 ml) cinnamon
Pinch nutmeg

RED PEPPER OIL:
3 red bell peppers, cut into 1-inch (2½ cm) cubes
2 cups (500 ml) extra-virgin olive oil

FENNEL AND APPLE SALAD: Using a mandolin, cut the fennel as thin as possible. Repeat with the apple. Mix together, "fluffing" the ingredients. Toss with the oil and juices. Season to taste.

HERB MOUSSE: Place the herbs, spinach and garlic in a blender and purée. Drizzle in the water and oil to make an emulsion. Purée again until super smooth. Season and store in the fridge. Can be made 1 day in advance.

CITRUS VINAIGRETTE: In a pot on low heat, reduce the juice by half. Blend all the ingredients together and season to taste.

SHRIMP: Season with salt and pepper and grill or sauté for 2 minutes on each side on medium heat. Slice in half lengthwise and drizzle with citrus vinaigrette.

CORIANDER TUILE: Heat oven to 325°F (160°C). In a large bowl, add the sugar and salt to the egg whites and whisk until foamy. Add the flour all at once and whisk again. Add the butter a little at a time, whisking well throughout. Whisk in the spices. Place a pencil-shaped line of mixture on parchment paper and cook for 4 minutes. While still warm, wrap around a chopstick.

RED PEPPER OIL: Place the peppers and oil in a heavy-bottomed pot. On medium-low heat, slowly simmer for 20 minutes, uncovered. Transfer to a bowl, cover and let sit for 10 minutes. Using a blender set at high, emulsify the oil and peppers. Cover and let rest overnight. The next day, decant the oil through a fine-mesh strainer. Can be stored in the fridge for 1 week.

TO ASSEMBLE: Arrange on individual plates. Drizzle some herb mousse down the centre of each plate. Top with the shrimp and fennel and apple salad, layered horizontally. Decorate with the coriander tuile and red pepper oil.

Serves 4

Chef's note: Only a bit of red pepper oil is needed for decoration. The reason for making such a large quantity is that it is difficult to make a smaller amount. It is great drizzled on top of grilled meat, fish or vegetables. The citrus vinaigrette is also used only in a small amount, but the leftover vinaigrette will be delicious on any salad. Will keep for 1 week in the fridge.

Nutritional Value Per Serving (437 g): Calories 752, Protein 5 g, Carbohydrates 27 g, Dietary Fibre 4.5 g, Sugars 116 g, Total Fat 45 g, Saturated Fat 9 g, Cholesterol 22 mg, Sodium 291 mg

SUGGESTED WINE PAIRING:
Inniskillin Winemaker's Barrel Aged Pinot Gris
Fresh peach, lime, honey and floral notes on the nose.
Floral and lime notes accented by a hint of spice are carried through a long smooth finish.

Blood Orange

Beef Carpaccio with Raw Asparagus, Blood Orange, Fennel and Endive Lettuces

12 oz (340 g) very fresh beef filet, centre cut

½ cup (125 ml) best-quality hazelnut oil

1 small fennel bulb

8 large asparagus tips, 4 inches (10 cm) long, cut into thin slices lengthwise

2 Italian blood oranges, segmented

Endive lettuces of choice

3 oz (85 g) hazelnuts, toasted and coarsely crushed

1 lemon, cut into wedges

Chunk of Parmesan cheese

Maldon sea salt and freshly ground pepper

Trim the filet of any surface discoloration. Wrap and chill well. Cut into ¼-inch (6 mm) slices and brush 1 side of each slice lightly with hazelnut oil. Place a slice of filet between 2 sheets of plastic wrap. Working from the centre, gently pound the filet using a flat mallet until it reaches a thickness of ⅛ inch (3 mm). Transfer to a serving plate and cover tightly with fresh plastic wrap, pushing it against the meat to remove any air. Refrigerate. Repeat with remaining slices, arranging the slices over the plates. This can be done up to 5 hours in advance of serving.

Cut the fennel into quarters. Trim the core if necessary but leave enough to keep the layers together. Shave into thin slices and drop into ice water to crisp for no more than 5 minutes. Take the plates from the fridge. Remove the plastic and season with salt and pepper. Top with a few fennel shavings, asparagus slices, orange segments and endive leaves, taking care not to overwhelm the beef. Sprinkle with the hazelnuts and a little more salt. Add a drizzle of hazelnut oil and a squeeze of lemon juice. Shave some Parmesan over each plate and serve immediately, while still chilled.

Serves 6

Nutritional Value Per Serving (211 g): Calories 417, Protein 19 g, Carbohydrates 12 g, Dietary Fibre 4.2 g, Sugars 5.2 g, Total Fat 33.2 g, Saturated Fat 4.8 g, Cholesterol 49 mg, Sodium 156 mg

fennel endive

SUGGESTED WINE PAIRING:
Masi Campofiorin 2006 5-Star Vintage
Rich, full-bodied, round and velvety
www.masi.it

Scallop Carpaccio with Citrus-Truffle Vinaigrette and Crisp Prosciutto

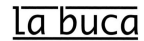

1 thin slice prosciutto di parma, about ½ oz (15 g)

2 scallops, fresh or thawed, about 1⅓ oz (40 g) each

2 tbsp (30 ml) extra-virgin olive oil

4 tsp (20 ml) Japanese soy sauce

2 tsp (10 ml) truffle oil

½ tsp (2 ml) truffle paste

Juice of ½ lemon

Small handful mixed herbs such as celery leaves, fennel fronds, snipped chives, Italian parsley

½ orange, in segments

Thinly sliced radish, to garnish

Heat oven to 400°F (200°C). Place the prosciutto between 2 sheets of parchment paper on a small baking tray and cook until crisp, about 5 minutes. Let cool. Slice each scallop into 5 coins and arrange on a serving dish. Put in the fridge. Whisking vigorously, combine the olive oil, soy sauce, truffle oil and paste and lemon juice. Toss the mixed herbs together and dress with 1 tsp (5 ml) of the vinaigrette. Remove the scallops from the fridge and drizzle with the remaining vinaigrette. Arrange the orange segments over the scallops and top with the prosciutto. Scatter the herb salad over the prosciutto and add the garnish. Serve immediately.

Serves 2

Nutritional Value Per Serving (130 g): Calories 305, Protein 10 g, Carbohydrates 7.2 g, Dietary Fibre 0.83 g, Sugars 4.5 g, Total Fat 26.7 g, Saturated Fat 3.8 g, Cholesterol 19 mg, Sodium 1155 mg

truffle oil orange

Qualicum Bay Scallops with Black Truffle Crust and Pancetta-Wrapped Porcini Mushrooms

CinCin

12 large Qualicum Bay scallops

2 tbsp (30 ml) olive oil

Garnishes: fresh-cooked peas, high-quality olive oil, aged balsamic vinegar, chopped chervil

BLACK TRUFFLE CRUST:

3 oz (85 g) dried black trumpet mushrooms

3 tbsp (45 ml) olive oil

2 shallots, chopped

2 garlic cloves, chopped

1 tsp (5 ml) thyme, chopped

⅓ cup (85 ml) dry white wine

1 cup (250 ml) butter

2 tsp (10 ml) Dijon mustard

2 tsp (10 ml) roasted garlic purée

2 cups (500 ml) panko (see note)

3 oz (85 g) high-quality truffle paste

3 tbsp (45 ml) black truffle oil, or white

Freshly squeezed lemon juice

Salt and freshly ground pepper

CAULIFLOWER PURÉE:

1 head cauliflower, roughly chopped

2 cups (500 ml) 35% cream

1 bunch thyme

PANCETTA-WRAPPED PORCINI:

12 medium-size porcini mushrooms, or 6 larger cut in half

2 tbsp (30 ml) extra-virgin olive oil

12 slices pancetta

ROASTED GARLIC PURÉE: Heat oven to 375°F (190°C). Cut a head of garlic in half across the middle and wrap in foil. Bake for 35 to 40 minutes. When cool enough to handle, squeeze out the garlic.

BLACK TRUFFLE CRUST: Soak the mushrooms in hot water for 15 to 20 minutes, then drain. Heat a stainless steel pan over medium-high heat and add the olive oil and mushrooms and sauté until soft. Stir in the shallots, garlic and thyme and cook for another 2 to 3 minutes. Deglaze with the wine and reduce. In another pan, brown the butter over medium heat, whisking continuously. Transfer the mushroom-shallot mixture and brown butter to a blender. Add the mustard and garlic purée and combine using the pulse setting. Transfer to a stainless steel bowl and use a spatula to fold in the panko, truffle paste, truffle oil and lemon juice. Season with salt and pepper to taste. Spread over a baking sheet and freeze for 1 hour. Using a round cookie cutter similar in size to the scallops, cut out 12 discs and set aside.

CAULIFLOWER PURÉE: Add cauliflower to a pot of boiling salted water and overcook. Strain. In a separate pan over medium heat, mix together cream and thyme and reduce until just over ½ cup (125 ml) remains. Strain and transfer to a food processor. Add the cauliflower and pulse until smooth. Pass through a sieve.

PANCETTA-WRAPPED PORCINI: Heat grill to high. Drizzle the mushrooms with about half the olive oil and season with salt and pepper. Place on grill for 1 minute on each side and set aside to cool. Wrap each mushroom with a slice of pancetta. Heat the remaining oil in a frying pan over medium-high heat and add the pancetta-wrapped mushrooms. Cook until the pancetta begins to crisp. Set aside in an ovenproof tray because you will put them in the oven later for 1 to 2 minutes, along with the scallops.

SCALLOPS: Turn the oven on to broil. Season the scallops with a pinch of salt. Heat the oil in a non-stick ovenproof frying pan over medium-high heat. Sear the scallops on 1 side, until golden-brown, then flip over and top the seared side with the mushroom discs. Place the pan in the oven and broil for 1 minute to set the discs. Put the pancetta-wrapped porcini in at the same time.

TO ASSEMBLE: Warm the plates first. Place 3 scallops and their truffle-crust toppings along the side of each plate. Spoon some cauliflower purée on the other side and top with peas, if using, and pancetta-wrapped porcini. Garnish and serve.

Serves 4

Chef's note: "Panko" means Japanese bread crumbs, which are very good in this recipe, but if you can't find them, regular bread crumbs will do. If you're wondering what's under the scallops in the picture, it's red beet purée, which acts as a perfect foil for the porcini.

Nutritional Value Per Serving (480 g): Calories 1161, Protein 29 g, Carbohydrates 15 g, Dietary Fibre 6.2 g, Sugars 5.3 g, Total Fat 98 g, Saturated Fat 49 g, Cholesterol 272 mg, Sodium 1288 mg

SUGGESTED WINE PAIRING:
Sumac Ridge Steller's Jay Brut
One of Canada's premier sparkling wines.
A well orchestrated blend of Chardonnay, Pinot Noir and Pinot Blanc.

Tuna Nachos

3 wonton wrappers, cut in half

Vegetable oil for deep-frying

2 oz (60 g) sashimi-grade tuna such as bigeye or yellowfin, chopped

¼ ripe avocado, cut into small cubes

1 green onion, finely chopped

1 jalapeno pepper, with seeds, finely sliced

¾ oz (20 g) tobiko (flying fish roe)

Garnishes: kaiware (Japanese radish sprouts), toasted sesame seeds

SAUCE:

1 tbsp (15 ml) kewpie (Japanese mayonnaise)

½ tsp (2 ml) sesame oil

½ tsp (2 ml) soy sauce

¼ tsp (1 ml) sriracha chili sauce

Heat about 2 inches (5 cm) of oil in a frying pan over medium heat. While oil is heating, mix all the sauce ingredients together in a medium bowl. Add the tuna, avocado and green onion to the sauce and toss to combine. Fry the wonton wrappers for about 40 seconds, until golden-brown, then drain on paper towel. Arrange 3 "nacho chips" on each plate and top with a dollop of the mixture. Place a jalapeno slice on top and some tobiko. Garnish and serve.

Serves 2

Chef's note: Can fry wonton wrappers 4 hours in advance.

Substitution: Instead of using fried wontons, use fresh endives or lettuce leaves as the base for the mixture.

Nutritional Value Per Serving (112 g): Calories 225, Protein 10 g, Carbohydrates 14 g, Dietary Fibre 2.2 g, Sugars 1.4 g, Total Fat 14.8 g, Saturated Fat 2.2 g, Cholesterol 16 mg, Sodium 271 mg

sesame oil
jalapeno

Avocado

Salmon Tartare
with Southwest Spices

Taverne
SUR LE SQUARE

10 oz (300 g) very fresh salmon, skin removed

1 ripe avocado

¼ cup plus 1 tbsp (80 ml) lime juice

2 tbsp (30 ml) chopped shallots

1 tbsp (15 ml) chopped cilantro

1½ tsp (7 ml) chopped chives

¼ cup (65 ml) olive oil

1½ tsp (7 ml) chipotle oil *(see note)*

¼ tsp (1 ml) fine salt

Soft tortillas, to make chips

To make the tortilla chips, cut the tortillas into triangles and bake on a silicone sheet in a 400°F (200°C) oven until crispy.

Dice the salmon and avocado into ¼-inch (6 mm) pieces and place in separate bowls. Season the avocado with salt and 1 tbsp (15 ml) of the lime juice and set aside. Add all other ingredients to the salmon and mix well. Check seasoning and add more salt, lime juice or other ingredients as necessary. Divide the avocado among the plates and top with the salmon tartare. Add some tortilla chips to each plate.

Chef's note: If you can't find chipotle oil, any other spice paste or oil can be used, such as ¼ to ½ tsp (1 to 2 ml) sriracha paste. The presentation is made more attractive with a few plate garnishes, such as balsamic vinegar or chive oil, made by blanching 1 bunch of chives, cooling in an ice bath, puréeing with olive oil and straining through a sieve.

Serves 4

Nutritional Value Per Serving (193 g): Calories 391, Protein 18 g, Carbohydrates 18 g, Dietary Fibre 4 g, Sugars 1.5 g, Total Fat 28 g, Saturated Fat 4 g, Cholesterol 41 mg, Sodium 294 mg

SUGGESTED WINE PAIRING:
Inniskillin Reserve Reisling
Delicate floral and honey aromas.
Pronounced citrus and apple notes and crisp acidity
combine for an extended finish on this elegant wine.

Albacore Tuna Pizza with Pesto, Crème Fraîche and Arugula

7 oz (200 g) fresh albacore tuna, thinly sliced

½ cup (125 ml) crème fraîche (see note)

Large handful arugula or other spicy green

PESTO:

2 small packages basil

½ cup (125 ml) pine nuts

½ cup (125 ml) grated Grana Padano cheese

1 garlic clove

¼ cup (65 ml) extra-virgin olive oil

Salt and freshly ground pepper

PIZZA DOUGH:

1½ oz (45 g) fresh yeast (if using dry,
half the amount)

½ cup plus 2 tbsp (155 ml) warm water

9 oz (250 g) flour

3 tbsp plus 1 tsp (50 ml) extra-virgin olive oil

Pinch salt

Extra-virgin olive oil, for greasing and drizzling

Cornmeal, for dusting

PESTO: Combine the basil, pine nuts, cheese and garlic in a food processor. With the machine running, add the olive oil until the consistency is almost liquid. Season to taste with salt and pepper.

PIZZA DOUGH: Heat oven to 500°F (260°C). Grease a baking sheet with oil and dust with cornmeal. Crumble the fresh yeast into the warm water and stir to dissolve. In a large bowl, combine the flour, olive oil and salt and stir in the yeast-water mixture. Once combined, continue mixing by hand for about 5 minutes, using a folding motion (the dough will be too wet to knead; this step can also be done in a standing mixer with a dough hook). Cover with plastic wrap or a moist kitchen towel and set in a warm place so the dough can double in size. Room temperature works fine but 100°F (38°C) is better.

Once the dough has doubled, punch it down to its original size and spread over the baking sheet using your hands. If it sticks to your hands, grease them with a bit of oil. Cook for about 5 minutes, until golden-brown and cooked through. Press the crust down if it puffs up. Let cool slightly before spreading with pesto. Arrange tuna on top and season with salt and pepper. Return to oven just long enough to warm but not cook the tuna. Cut into slices and drizzle with the crème fraîche. Add a scattering of arugula leaves and a splash of olive oil.

Serves 2

Chef's note: To prepare the crème fraîche, you need a 1:3 ratio of buttermilk to whipping cream. Mix together and let stand on your counter for 24 hours, then refrigerate. If you don't have time for this step, sour cream can be used instead.

Nutritional Value Per Serving (678 g): Calories 1539, Protein 62 g, Carbohydrates 111 g, Dietary Fibre 9.6 g, Sugars 3.6 g, Total Fat 94 g, Saturated Fat 19 g, Cholesterol 102 mg, Sodium 960 mg

Œuf Poché with Asparagus and Pickled Mushrooms

1 egg, soft poached

5 white or green asparagus spears, blanched

1 1-inch-thick (2½ cm) slice brioche or baguette, toasted, or use your favourite bread

1 cup (250 ml) lettuce leaves and delicate herbs such as chervil, tarragon, dill or chives

1-2 tbsp (15-30 ml) pickled mushrooms

1 tbsp (15 ml) truffle or olive oil

1 tbsp (15 ml) port wine vinaigrette

PICKLED MUSHROOMS:

1 cup (250 ml) small mushrooms such as honey, cinnamon cap, black trumpet, beach, oyster or shiitake; even dried mushrooms can be used

1 cup (250 ml) champagne, tarragon or white wine vinegar

½ cup (125 ml) water

¼ cup (65 ml) sugar

4 cloves

2 sprigs fresh tarragon

1 shallot, finely sliced

1 bay leaf

Salt and freshly ground pepper

PORT WINE VINAIGRETTE:

2 cups (500 ml) port wine

1 tbsp (15 ml) honey

2 shallots, minced

Splash red wine vinegar

PICKLED MUSHROOMS: Place the mushrooms in a bowl. In a medium saucepan, bring all the other ingredients to a boil. Pour the hot liquid over the mushrooms and let cool. Cover and store in refrigerator. Can be made up to 1 week in advance.

PORT WINE VINAIGRETTE: Place all the ingredients in a non-reactive saucepan and heat over low until the liquid is reduced to a marmalade-like consistency. Adjust seasoning and acidity by adding more vinegar, salt or pepper. Can be made up to 6 days in advance.

TO ASSEMBLE: Keep the toast and asparagus warm in the oven while you poach the egg to the desired doneness. When the egg is ready, place the toast on a warm plate and lay the asparagus on top. Garnish the plate with the lettuce leaves, fine herbs and pickled mushrooms. Drizzle with the truffle oil and port wine vinaigrette. Arrange the poached egg on the asparagus and serve.

Serves 1

Chef's note: This dish is great with any kind of egg, including scrambled, fried or hard-boiled.

Nutritional Value Per Serving (315 g): Calories 445, Protein 16 g, Carbohydrates 48 g, Dietary Fibre 4.9 g, Sugars 8.1 g, Total Fat 19.7 g, Saturated Fat 3.7 g, Cholesterol 185 mg, Sodium 570 mg

Beef Tartare

1 lb (450 g) beef tenderloin, cleaned and finely chopped

2 shallots, finely diced

2 tbsp (30 ml) capers, roughly chopped

1 bunch chives, finely sliced

2 tbsp (30 ml) extra-virgin olive oil

1 tsp (5 ml) truffle oil

2 egg yolks

1 tbsp (15 ml) Worcestershire

1 tsp (5 ml) Dijon mustard

A couple shakes of Tabasco

Salt and freshly ground pepper

Watercress, to garnish

Combine all the ingredients in a bowl until well incorporated. Serve within the hour. Don't put in the fridge because the meat will oxidize and change colour.

Excellent accompanied by crostini, crackers or French fries.

Serves 4

Nutritional Value Per Serving (140 g): Calories 345, Protein 33 g, Carbohydrates 0.7 g, Dietary Fibre 0.01 g, Sugars 0.09 g, Total Fat 23 g, Saturated Fat 6.8 g, Cholesterol 199 mg, Sodium 253 mg

Shiitake

Braised Bacon Burgundy-Style
with Marinated Mushrooms
and Onions and Red Wine Jelly

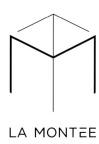

LA MONTÉE

18 oz (500 g) smoked bacon, not sliced

¾ cup plus 1½ tbsp (200 ml) red wine, any type

MARINATED MUSHROOMS AND ONIONS:

3½ oz (100 g) mushrooms, could be shiitake, oyster, Paris or any kind, cut into quarters

5 small white onions, sliced

½ cup plus 2 tbsp (150 ml) red wine vinegar

½ cup plus 2 tbsp (150 ml) sugar

½ cup plus 2 tbsp (150 ml) water

Sprinkling of fresh chives, sliced small

Salt and freshly ground pepper

RED WINE GELATIN:

1½ gelatin sheets, or 1 oz (3 g) gelatin powder

MARINATED MUSHROOMS AND ONIONS: Prepare this the night before. Place the mushrooms and onions in 2 separate containers. Bring the red wine vinegar, sugar and water to a boil and immediately pour equally into the containers. Add chives to both and season with salt and pepper.

BRAISED BACON: Heat oven to 350°F (180°C). Put the bacon in a roasting pan and add half the red wine and enough water to cover. Braise for 2 hours, covered with a piece of foil, basting frequently with the liquid. Let cool and slice very thin, as you would bacon strips.

RED WINE GELATIN: While the bacon is braising, bring the other half of the red wine to a boil in a small pot. Season with salt and pepper to taste. Immediately pour the hot liquid over the gelatin and stir until melted. Pour into a small, flat-bottomed dish and let cool in the refrigerator until set, about 1 hour. Cut into small cubes.

TO ASSEMBLE: Place the sliced bacon on a hot plate and spoon the marinated vegetables on top. Sprinkle with the gelatin cubes.

Serves 4 to 5

Nutritional Value Per Serving (389 g): Calories 785, Protein 38 g, Carbohydrates 33 g, Dietary Fibre 1.8 g, Sugars 26.9 g, Total Fat 53 g, Saturated Fat 17.9 g, Cholesterol 134 mg, Sodium 2671 mg

Lentil and Goat Cheese Bruschetta

2 cups (500 ml) Dupuy lentils

2 cups (500 ml) red wine

2 cups (500 ml) veal stock

2 cups mirepoix *(see note)*

1 4-oz (125 g) piece bacon (optional)

4 thick slices day-old bread

1½ cups (375 ml) olive oil

12 olive-poached cherry tomatoes

1 head garlic, roasted

4 large pieces Swiss chard, blanched

1 tsp (5 ml) butter

8 slices pancetta

4 heaping tbsp (about 80 g) fresh goat cheese

Maldon salt and freshly ground pepper

Grape must, known as vincotto, to garnish

ROASTED GARLIC: Heat oven to 400°F (200°C). Slice off the top of the garlic head and wrap in foil. Bake until soft, about 45 minutes. Squeeze out garlic and reserve.

Place the lentils, red wine, veal stock, mirepoix and bacon in a saucepan and bring to a boil. Reduce heat and let simmer, uncovered, for 45 minutes, or until the lentils are tender. Drain, reserving the liquid, and then reduce the liquid by three-quarters, until thick. While the lentils are cooking, sauté the day-old bread in about ½ cup (125 ml) of olive oil. Let cool and become hard. To poach the tomatoes, place about 1 cup (250 ml) of olive oil in a pan to cover the tomatoes. Heat the oil on medium and when hot, toss in the tomatoes. Remove just when the skin begins to crack. (Save the oil for another use.) Prepare the pancetta by frying in a pan or cooking in a 350°F (180°C) oven on a baking sheet for about 15 minutes.

TO ASSEMBLE: Place some of the reduced liquid in a saucepan and add the lentils, cherry tomatoes and Swiss chard. Heat gently until warm and season with salt and pepper. Stir in the butter. Spread some roasted garlic and a generous dollop of goat cheese on each slice of bread, and then place in the oven at 350°F (180°C) for a few minutes, so the cheese melts just slightly and the bread is warm. Place a touch of goat cheese in the centre of each plate to prevent the bread from sliding. Place the warmed bread on the cheese and top with a couple slices of pancetta. Pour the lentil mixture on top and garnish with 1 tsp (5 ml) of vincotto.

Serves 4

Chef's note: A mirepoix is a mixture of finely diced onion, carrot and celery. For this recipe I use 1 cup (250 ml) onion and ½ cup (125 ml) each of carrot and celery.

Nutritional Value Per Serving (516 g): Calories 466, Protein 26 g, Carbohydrates 53 g, Dietary Fibre 13.5 g, Sugars 9.7 g, Total Fat 7.2 g, Saturated Fat 3.1 g, Cholesterol 28 mg, Sodium 1134 mg

Duck Spring Rolls

DUCK CONFIT:
4 duck legs
1 celery stalk, minced
1 medium carrot, minced
1 medium onion, minced
6 large garlic cloves, minced
¼ cup (65 ml) chopped cilantro
1 tbsp (15 ml) grated ginger
1 tsp (5 ml) crushed black peppercorns
¼ cup (65 ml) soy sauce
1 tbsp (15 ml) Marsala wine
1 tbsp (15 ml) sesame oil
2 tbsp (30 ml) salt
Vegetable oil to cover

SPRING ROLL FILLING:
Shredded duck confit
2 tbsp (30 ml) black sweet vinegar
¼ bunch cilantro, chopped
Juice of ½ lime
1 tbsp (15 ml) Sambal Oelek
Juice of 2 oranges *(see note)*

ASIAN SLAW:
¼ English cucumber, julienned
1 carrot, julienned
1 celery stalk, julienned
½ red onion, julienned
¼ cup (65 ml) white vinegar
¼ cup (65 ml) sugar
Pinch dry chilis

VERMICELLI RICE NOODLES:
4 oz (115 g) thin rice vermicelli
2 tbsp (30 ml) sesame oil
1 tsp (5 ml) salt

Segments from 2 peeled oranges
8-inch (22 cm) rice papers, or smaller ones for more spring rolls

GARNISHES: hoisin, Goma Shabu sauce or chili oil

DUCK CONFIT: Combine all the ingredients and marinate overnight. Remove legs from marinade and set in roasting pan. Cover with vegetable oil and cook, covered, in a 260°F (127°C) oven for 3 hours. Allow roasting pan to cool before removing legs. Wrap and refrigerate until ready to use, at which time place on a baking sheet and cook in a 400°F (200°C) oven, uncovered, for 5 minutes. Shred with a fork while warm and let cool before combining with other filling ingredients. ASIAN SLAW: Mix all the ingredients together and set aside to macerate for 10 to 20 minutes. VERMICELLI RICE NOODLES: Bring 8 cups (2 L) water to a boil. While waiting for the boil, soak vermicelli in hot water until it softens and can be pulled apart. Add the noodles to boiling water and cook for 20 seconds. Drain while running cool water over noodles. Once cooled, add the sesame oil and salt; mix well and adjust seasoning as necessary. Set aside. SOAKING THE RICE PAPERS: Fill a wide bowl with hot water. Working with 2 rice papers at a time, put in hot water until they begin to soften. Hang to dry on the outside edge of a different bowl until they become pliable and sticky.

TO ASSEMBLE: Place a rice paper on a plate. Add some of the noodles to the lower centre of the paper. Top with an equal amount of the Asian slaw, and on top of that an equal amount of duck filling. Add 2 orange segments side by side. To roll, fold the right and left sides over the filling and roll from the bottom to the top. Finish with a drizzle of hoisin or Goma Shabu sauce or chili oil.

Serves 6 to 10

Chef's note: Peel the oranges by slicing off the top and bottom, then removing the outside by cutting from top to bottom. Remove each segment with a pairing knife, working over the bowl containing the duck confit to catch any juices. When finished separating the segments, squeeze the remaining pulp to ensure all the juice falls into the bowl. If you don't have the time to make your own duck confit, you can buy it ready-made at a specialty grocer.

Nutritional Value Per Serving (259 g): Calories 409, Protein 21 g, Carbohydrates 43 g, Dietary Fibre 2.7 g, Sugars 15.3 g, Total Fat 16.8 g, Saturated Fat 3.2 g, Cholesterol 70 mg, Sodium 1381 mg

Pan-Seared
Digby Scallops

Catch
RESTAURANT & OYSTER BAR

12 large Digby scallops

2 tbsp (30 ml) vegetable oil

Salt and freshly ground pepper

Garnishes: small salad of sliced radish and organic baby greens

RED WINE REDUCTION:

1 cup (250 ml) red wine

2 tbsp (30 ml) sugar

2 sprigs thyme

1 tbsp (15 ml) vegetable oil

2 tsp (10 ml) soy sauce

CARROT PURÉE:

1 large carrot, peeled and diced

1 tbsp (15 ml) chopped ginger

EDAMAME AND SNOW CRAB MASHED POTATO:

12 oz (340 g) Yukon gold potatoes, peeled and chopped

2 oz (60 g) edamame beans, cooked

2 oz (60 g) snow crab meat, cooked

6 tbsp (90 ml) 35% cream

2 tsp (10 ml) togarashi pepper (Japanese seven spice)

Prepare the red wine reduction by placing the red wine, sugar and thyme in a saucepan over medium heat. Reduce by about two-thirds and remove from heat. Add the vegetable oil and soy sauce. Strain. Keep warm until ready to serve. While the red wine mixture is reducing, make the carrot purée. Place the carrot and ginger in a saucepan and cover with salted water. Cook over medium heat until soft, then drain. Purée in a blender and season to taste with salt and pepper.

Make the potatoes by boiling in salted water on high heat, uncovered, until fork tender. Drain and mash by hand. Fold in the edamame beans and snow crab and season with togarashi pepper and salt. Cover and keep warm.

Heat a heavy-bottomed pan on high heat. While pan is heating, dust the scallops, top and bottom, with salt and pepper. When pan is hot, add the oil. Cook scallops on first side for 1 to 2 minutes, until a golden-brown crust has formed. Turn over and cook another minute. Remove from heat and leave in pan for a few minutes to continue warming the interior of the scallops.

Place some carrot purée on each plate and set a pile of mashed potatoes next to it. Top with seared scallops. Drizzle the red wine reduction around the plate, garnish and serve.

Serves 4

Nutritional Value Per Serving (278 g): Calories 369, Protein 15.5 g, Carbohydrates 30 g, Dietary Fibre 2.7 g, Sugars 7 g, Total Fat 16.7 g, Saturated Fat 6.3 g, Cholesterol 56 mg, Sodium 387 mg

SUGGESTED WINE PAIRING:
Dan Aykroyd Discovery Series Sauvignon Blanc
A beautiful match to light seafood dishes.
www.DanAykroydWines.com

Port,obello

Polenta con Funghi e Gorgonzola

daMaurizio
FINE · DINING

MUSHROOMS:

2 tbsp (30 ml) extra-virgin olive oil

1 tbsp (15 ml) butter

4 portobello mushroom caps,
cut in half and thinly sliced

16 shiitake mushrooms, stems removed
and coarsely chopped

Coarse salt and freshly ground pepper

2 tbsp (30 ml) balsamic vinegar

½ cup (125 ml) beef or chicken stock

2 scallions, thinly sliced on an angle

POLENTA:

3 cups (750 ml) chicken stock

1 cup (250 ml) quick-cooking polenta *(see note)*

2 tbsp (30 ml) butter

¼ cup (65 ml) grated Parmesan or
Romano, plus extra for garnish

¼ cup (65 ml) gorgonzola

GARNISHES:

White truffle oil

Thyme sprig

Bring the stock for the polenta to a boil in a covered pot. While waiting for it to boil, start preparing the mushrooms. Heat a large non-stick frying pan over medium-high heat and add the oil and butter. Throw in the mushrooms and season with salt and pepper to taste. Stirring frequently, cook for 10 minutes or until the mushrooms are dark and tender. Add the vinegar and stir to coat (it will evaporate in about 1 minute). Add the ½ cup (125 ml) stock and scallions and toss to combine.

Stir the quick-cooking polenta into the boiling chicken stock. Reduce heat to low and stir until it masses. Stir in the butter and cheese and season with salt and pepper. Serve with the mushrooms on top and garnished with a drizzle of white truffle oil, shaved Parmesan or Romano and a sprig of thyme.

Serves 4

Chef's note: You can find quick-cooking polenta in specialty food aisles at the supermarket or at Italian groceries. If you have demi-glace on hand, add ¼ cup (65 ml) to the mushrooms. Heating the oil and butter together prevents the butter from burning.

Nutritional Value Per Serving (428 g): Calories 418, Protein 12 g, Carbohydrates 45 g, Dietary Fibre 5.8 g, Sugars 4.3 g, Total Fat 21 g, Saturated Fat 9.3 g, Cholesterol 37 mg, Sodium 1094 mg

Morel Mushroom and Leek Tart

TART SHELL:

1 cup (250 ml) flour

½ cup (125 ml) cold butter

½ tsp (2 ml) salt

1 tbsp plus 2 tsp (25 ml) ice water

FILLING:

2½ cups (625 ml) sliced leeks

1 cup (250 ml) diced yellow onions

⅔ cup (170 ml) sliced shallots

1 tbsp (15 ml) minced garlic

2 tbsp (30 ml) butter

5½ oz (155 g) morel mushrooms, brushed and rinsed

Salt and freshly ground pepper

1 tbsp (15 ml) chopped parsley

TOPPING:

⅓ cup (85 ml) 35% cream

⅓ cup (85 ml) skim milk

1 whole egg

1 oz (30 g) Gouda, grated

Heat oven to 350°F (180°C). Combine the flour, butter and salt in a food processor until it has the consistency of a fine grain. Transfer to a bowl and add the water by hand, incorporating until smooth. Roll out to fit a shallow tart pan that measures 4½ by 13½ inches (12 by 34 cm). Cover with pie weights or dried beans and bake for 40 minutes. Remove the weights and bake for 10 minutes more, until golden-brown. Keep the oven on to bake the tart.

While the tart shell is baking, combine the leeks, onions, shallots, garlic and butter in a saucepan and sweat over medium-low heat until tender. Add the mushrooms and continue to cook until most of the liquid has dissipated. Season well with salt and pepper. Remove from heat and add the parsley.

To assemble, purée the cream, milk and egg in a blender for about 2 minutes. Spread the mushroom mixture evenly onto the warm tart shell. Fill the shell with the cream mixture and then sprinkle on the cheese. Bake for about 30 minutes or until the custard has set and the top has browned. Let stand for about 1 hour before cutting.

Suggested side dish: Grilled asparagus and tomatoes.

Serves 4 to 6

Nutritional Value Per Serving (299 g): Calories 576, Protein 11 g, Carbohydrates 44 g, Dietary Fibre 3 g, Sugars 6.7 g, Total Fat 40 g, Saturated Fat 25 g, Cholesterol 159 mg, Sodium 610 mg

Gouda

Soups

Leek

Mussel and Saffron Soup

¼ cup (65 ml) butter

1 medium onion, thinly sliced

¼ bunch thyme plus 1 tsp (5 ml) chopped thyme

2 lb (900 g) fresh cultivated mussels, scrubbed

1 cup (250 ml) dry white wine

1 cup (250 ml) 35% cream

Pinch best-quality saffron threads

1 small carrot, julienned, blanched and refreshed

Half a leek, julienned, blanched and refreshed

Over medium heat, melt the butter in a large saucepan that has a tight-fitting lid. Add the onion and bunch of thyme and cook for a few minutes, until fragrant. Add the mussels and wine, cover the pan and turn the heat to high. After about 2 minutes turn the mussels over with a large spoon, bringing the bottom ones to the top. Cover again and cook until they have just opened. The whole process should take about 4 minutes.

Tip the mussels into a colander set over a bowl to catch every drop of liquid. When cool enough to handle, remove the mussels from their shells and reserve on a plate. Cover with a damp towel to prevent from drying. Discard the onion and thyme. Strain the liquid into a pot through a fine cloth to remove any sand. Add the cream to the liquid along with the saffron and chopped thyme. Bring to a boil. Remove from heat and correct the seasoning. Divide among serving bowls and arrange the cooked mussels in each bowl, stuffing a few into 1 or 2 shells, if desired. Top with the julienned carrots and leek and serve.

Serves 12 to 14

Nutritional Value Per Serving (138 g): Calories 195, Protein 9.7 g, Carbohydrates 5.8 g, Dietary Fibre 0.43 g, Sugars 0.95 g, Total Fat 13.4 g, Saturated Fat 7.6 g, Cholesterol 59.8 mg, Sodium 259 mg

SUGGESTED WINE PAIRING:
Jackson-Triggs Proprietors' Grand Reserve Methode Classique
Named Top Winery in Canada an unprecedented 20 times in global competitions
Awarded Bronze in the Challenge International du Vin in Bordeaux, France
Concentrated vanilla, citrus and floral aromas with subtle toasty nuances

Acquacotta
The Stone Soup of Italy

Mistura

1 large white onion, chopped very fine

½ cup (125 ml) minced celery

4 garlic cloves, crushed, plus another clove for flavouring the bread

¼ cup (65 ml) extra-virgin olive oil

3 cups (750 ml) canned plum tomatoes, seeds removed

4 cups (1 L) vegetable stock

1 bunch basil, chopped

Kosher salt and freshly ground pepper

4 eggs

1 cup (250 ml) grated pecorino cheese

4 slices country-style bread, toasted and rubbed with cut side of half a garlic clove

In a soup pot, heat the oil on medium. Add the onions, celery and garlic and cook until translucent, 4 to 5 minutes, stirring occasionally. Stir in the tomatoes and continue to cook for a few minutes, leaving the pot uncovered. Add the stock and basil and bring to a simmer. Let simmer for about 15 minutes. Season with salt and pepper. Reduce heat to low.

Crack 1 of the eggs into a small bowl, making sure the yolk doesn't break. Slowly add it to the hot soup. Do not stir. Repeat this process with each egg. When all the eggs are in, cook the soup for 1 more minute, covered. Ladle into bowls, placing 1 egg in each bowl. Top with a generous sprinkling of the pecorino and a drizzle of extra-virgin olive oil. Finish the soup by laying a slice of toast in each bowl.

Serves 4

Nutritional Value Per Serving (655 g): Calories 601, Protein 28 g, Carbohydrates 57 g, Dietary Fibre 5.7 g, Sugars 14.5 g, Total Fat 30 g, Saturated Fat 10 g, Cholesterol 219 mg, Sodium 4570 mg

Yucatan
Hot and Sour Soup

6 cups (1½ L) chicken stock

1 jalapeno pepper

¼ bunch coriander, tied with a string

2 smoked chicken breasts, pulled into bite-size pieces *(see note)*

¼ cup (65 ml) goji berries

2 green onions, thinly sliced into rounds

¼ cup (65 ml) coarsely chopped coriander

½ cup (125 ml) cooked orzo

¼ cup (65 ml) lime juice

Salt

Garnish: edible flowers

Slice the jalapeno in half lengthwise and gently bruise both halves with the heel of a knife. Place the stock in a pot set over medium heat. Add the jalapeno and coriander and bring to just under a simmer. Turn the heat to low, cover the pot and let the stock infuse for half an hour. Remove the jalapeno and coriander. While the stock is infusing, divide the chicken, goji berries, green onions, coriander and orzo equally among the heated bowls. Finish the soup by adding the lime juice. If you prefer a more sour flavour, add more lime juice. Adjust the seasoning with salt to taste and ladle the soup into the bowls. Top with the garnish.

Serves 4

Chef's note: Smoked chicken breasts can be purchased at most grocery stores and specialty markets.

Nutritional Value Per Serving (439 g): Calories 178, Protein 18 g, Carbohydrates 19.5 g, Dietary Fibre 1.9 g, Sugars 2.1 g, Total Fat 2.9 g, Saturated Fat 0.2 g, Cholesterol 34 mg, Sodium 1561 mg

SUGGESTED WINE PAIRING:
Villa Sandi Prosecco
a refreshing sparkling wine from Veneto, Italy
www.pmwine.com

Sea Urchins in a Cucumber Vichyssoise

4 medium-size sea urchins

CUCUMBER VICHYSSOISE:

3 tbsp (45 ml) unsalted butter

3 leeks, whites only, thinly sliced

½ small onion, thinly sliced

3½ oz (100 g) potatoes, diced

2 cups (500 ml) chicken stock

¾ cup (190 ml) 18% cream

1 English cucumber, peeled, seeded and sliced

GARNISH:

1 tbsp (15 ml) cucumber brunoise *(see note)*

1 tbsp (15 ml) minced chives

SEA URCHINS: Place a small cutting board in the centre of a baking sheet. Wearing gloves, 1 at a time place a sea urchin mouth-side up on the cutting board and crack it open with a heavy chef's knife, making sure not to cut through it completely. Use a solid pair of shears to cut a 1-inch (2½ cm) circle around the mouth. With a teaspoon, carefully remove the roe and wash in a bowl of cold salted water to remove any grit. Place the roe on a paper towel and refrigerate until needed.

CUCUMBER VICHYSSOISE: In a medium pot, melt the butter over medium-high heat and sweat the leeks and onion with a good pinch of salt and several turns of pepper for about 5 minutes, or until tender but not browned. Add potatoes and chicken stock and simmer for 20 minutes, uncovered, until potatoes are tender. Add the cream. Purée the mixture in a food processor while gradually adding the cucumber slices. Pass through a medium-mesh strainer. Season to taste with salt and pepper and refrigerate until well chilled. To serve, ladle about ¾ cup (190 ml) of the vichyssoise into each bowl. Place 5 pieces of sea urchin roe (or 3 oysters) on top of the soup. Garnish with cucumber brunoise and minced chives.

Serves 4

Chef's note: Vichyssoise is a creamy French-style soup that is traditionally served cold. Preparing the sea urchins can be a bit messy, so wear an apron and work over a baking sheet with a generous lip to catch all the juices. To make the cucumber brunoise, dice the cucumber into tiny cubes about ⅛ inch (3 mm) in size.

Substitution: Whole sea urchins or trays of sea urchin roe are available at Japanese specialty stores that offer fresh seafood, but if you can't find them, 12 Kusshi oysters can be used instead. Chuck with oyster knife and remove the shells. Drain and reserve in the fridge.

Nutritional Value Per Serving (462 g): Calories 335, Protein 18 g, Carbohydrates 25 g, Dietary Fibre 2.3 g, Sugars 4.2 g, Total Fat 18 g, Saturated Fat 9.5 g, Cholesterol 115 mg, Sodium 721 mg

chives

Chilled Velouté of English Peas with Goat Cheese and Elderflower Cream

VELOUTÉ:

1 medium onion, chopped

½ garlic clove, sliced

2 tbsp (30 ml) olive oil

18 oz (500 g) fresh or frozen peas, blanched

7 oz (200 g) vegetable stock

9 oz (250 g) arugula

ELDERFLOWER CREAM:

⅓ cup (85 ml) 4% milk

1 gelatin sheet

5 oz (150 g) soft goat cheese

1 tbsp (15 ml) elderflower cordial

1 egg white, lightly whipped

Pinch espelette pepper

GARNISHES:

¼ cup (65 ml) fresh peas, split and peeled

Handful pea shoots

VELOUTÉ: In a heavy-bottomed medium-size saucepan, heat the olive oil over medium heat. Add the onion and garlic and cook gently until soft, making sure not to colour. Add the peas and vegetable stock, cover and bring to a simmer. Cook for 4 to 5 minutes. Transfer to a blender, add the arugula and purée. Pass the mixture through a sieve. Check seasoning and chill over ice.

ELDERFLOWER CREAM: In a small saucepan, warm the milk over medium heat, then dissolve the gelatin sheet. In a bowl, break the goat cheese with a spatula until soft and smooth. Add the elderflower cordial to the cheese, followed by the milk-gelatin blend, mixing continuously. Gently fold in the whipped egg white. Season with the espelette pepper. Let set in the refrigerator for about 1 hour.

TO ASSEMBLE: Using a dessert spoon, smooth the elderflower cream around the inside upper edge of each bowl. Arrange the garnish of peas and pea shoots at the bottom. Gently pour the chilled velouté around the garnish.

Serves 4

Nutritional Value Per Serving (368 g): Calories 339, Protein 20 g, Carbohydrates 31 g, Dietary Fibre 8.2 g, Sugars 12.5 g, Total Fat 16 g, Saturated Fat 6.9 g, Cholesterol 20 mg, Sodium 848 mg

Roasted Butternut Squash Soup
with Moroccan-Spiced Squash Seeds

½ cup (125 ml) butter

2 yellow onions, sliced

2 celery stalks, sliced

2 large butternut squash, peeled, seeded and diced, seeds reserved

Small bunch thyme, tied with string

Salt and freshly ground pepper

Olive oil, for drizzling and coating the seeds

RAS AL HANOUT SPICE MIXTURE:

3 tbsp (45 ml) paprika

3 tbsp (45 ml) cinnamon

2½ tbsp (37 ml) ground cumin

2 tbsp (30 ml) turmeric

1½ tbsp (22 ml) ground mustard seed

1 tbsp (15 ml) ground coriander

2½ tsp (12 ml) ginger

2 tsp (10 ml) nutmeg

1½ tsp (7 ml) ground fennel

1 tsp (5 ml) ground chili flakes

20 whole cloves, ground

To make the soup, melt the butter over medium heat in a large pot and sweat the onions and celery until soft, about 5 minutes. Add the squash and thyme bundle and season with a bit of salt and pepper. Cover and sweat the squash until the edges start to dissolve, stirring from time to time. This should take about 10 minutes. Add just enough water to cover and bring to a boil. Reduce heat to a simmer, season again lightly and cook, uncovered, for about 20 minutes, until vegetables are very soft. Remove the thyme and purée the mixture in a blender, adding water if too thick. For a more refined texture, pass through a fine-mesh strainer. Check for seasoning. Ladle into bowls and top with the spiced seeds and a drizzle of olive oil.

SPICED SEEDS: Prepare while the soup is cooking. Rinse the seeds well to remove any squash meat and dry on a paper towel. Toss in a bit of olive oil and toast in a frying pan in the oven at 350°F (180°C) until golden-brown. While seeds are toasting, combine the spices for the ras al hanout. While still warm, season with salt and pepper and a dash of the spice mixture.

Serves 4

Substitution: If you don't have time to make the ras al hanout, use curry or chili powder instead. The ras al hanout can be stored for several months in an airtight container at room temperature.

Nutritional Value Per Serving (245 g): Calories 399, Protein 6.2 g, Carbohydrates 38 g, Dietary Fibre 15.7 g, Sugars 5.7 g, Total Fat 28 g, Saturated Fat 15 g, Cholesterol 61 mg, Sodium 301 mg

Ginger

Hot and Sour Duck Broth
with Duck Meatballs and Scallions

BROTH:

1 duck carcass

3 tbsp (45 ml) canola oil

2 onions, sliced

2 carrots, sliced

1 leek, whites only, sliced

5 garlic cloves, sliced

2 tbsp (30 ml) minced ginger

1 lemongrass stalk, sliced

8 cups (2 L) chicken stock, salt-free or low-sodium

2 tbsp (30 ml) sriracha

¼ cup (65 ml) red wine vinegar

¼ cup (65 ml) soy sauce

Salt and freshly ground pepper

DUCK MEATBALLS:

1 duck breast, ground with fat, about 1 lb (450 g)

1 chicken breast, ground, about 7 oz (200 g)

2 slices bacon, ground

1 tbsp (15 ml) minced ginger

1 tbsp (15 ml) minced garlic

1 egg yolk

¼ cup (65 ml) bread crumbs

1 tbsp (15 ml) Worcestershire

½ tsp (2 ml) Tabasco

Sliced scallions, to garnish

BROTH: Heat oven to 400°F (200°C). Roast the duck carcass, uncovered, until nicely browned, about 1 hour. In a soup pot on low heat, add the oil and sweat the onions, carrots, leek, garlic, ginger and lemongrass for about 5 minutes, making sure not to brown. Add the chicken stock and simmer for about 45 minutes, uncovered. Strain through a sieve and return the broth to the pot. Put over low heat and add the sriracha, red wine vinegar and soy sauce. Season with salt and pepper to taste.

DUCK MEATBALLS: Mix all the ingredients together and form into small meatballs. Over low heat, poach the meatballs in the broth for 4 to 5 minutes. Garnish the soup with the scallions.

Substitution: If you can't find a duck carcass, replace with chicken.

Serves 8

Nutritional Value Per Serving (411 g): Calories 238, Protein 24 g, Carbohydrates 10.7 g, Dietary Fibre 1.3 g, Sugars 4 g, Total Fat 10.8 g, Saturated Fat 2 g, Cholesterol 102 mg, Sodium 1625 mg

Minestrone al Pesto

MINESTRONE:

1½ cups (375 ml) pinto beans

1½ cups (375 ml) white beans

4 canned plum tomatoes,
cut into ½-inch (12 mm) dice

4 celery stalks,
cut into ½-inch (12 mm) slices

2 medium zucchini,
cut into ½-inch (12 mm) moons

2 potatoes, peeled and
cut into ½-inch (12 mm) dice

2 leeks, cut into ½-inch (12 mm) moons

2 asparagus spears, sliced

1 medium red onion, cut into medium dice

½ cup (125 ml) fresh or frozen peas

4 tbsp (60 ml) extra-virgin olive oil

4 cups (1 L) low-sodium chicken stock

6 oz (170 g) small pasta shells

Salt and freshly ground pepper

PESTO:

3 tbsp (45 ml) pine nuts

2 cups (500 ml) basil leaves,
preferably fine baby leaves

1 garlic clove

Pinch sea salt

½ cup plus 2 tbsp (155 ml)
extra-virgin olive oil

To make the pesto, place the pine nuts, basil, garlic and salt in a food processor and process until a paste forms, or this can be done by hand with a pestle and mortar. Add the olive oil and incorporate. Can be stored in a jar in the fridge, topped with extra-virgin olive oil, for up to 1 week.

To make the minestrone, start by soaking the pinto and white beans separately overnight. Drain. In a large soup pot, combine both beans with the tomato, celery, zucchini, potato, leek, asparagus, onion, peas and olive oil. Add enough chicken stock to submerge the vegetables by 1 inch (2½ cm) and season with salt and pepper. Cover and bring to a boil. Lower heat and simmer until the beans are tender, between 1 and 1½ hours. Add the pasta and turn the heat to high. Cook at a boil until al dente. Divide the soup among the bowls and top each bowl with a dollop of pesto.

Serves 4 to 8

Nutritional Value Per Serving (851 g): Calories 1191, Protein 38 g, Carbohydrates 101 g, Dietary Fibre 17.6 g, Sugars 11.6 g, Total Fat 73 g, Saturated Fat 11 g, Cholesterol 23 mg, Sodium 888 mg

Spring Asparagus and Brown Beech Mushroom Soup with Great Northern Beans

1-inch (2½ cm) piece ginger, minced

1 garlic clove, minced

1 small shallot, minced

1 medium-size fennel bulb, trimmed and minced

1 tbsp (15 ml) vegetable oil

8 cups (2 L) cold water

1 sprig thyme, chopped

1 tsp (5 ml) lemon juice

1 tsp (5 ml) grainy mustard

2 cups (500 ml) Great Northern beans, cooked

SACHET:

½ tsp (2 ml) whole black peppercorns

1 bay leaf

3-4 juniper berries

½ yellow onion, chopped

½ carrot, chopped

18 oz (500 g) brown beech mushrooms (about 2 clusters)

1 tbsp (15 ml) vegetable oil

Sea salt and freshly ground pepper

24 asparagus spears

In a large saucepan, sauté the ginger, garlic, shallot and fennel in the oil over medium heat for 10 minutes, or until tender. Be careful not to brown. Place the peppercorns, bay leaf, juniper, onion and carrot in a piece of cheesecloth and tie it up to make a sachet. Add the water, thyme, lemon juice, mustard, beans and the sachet to the saucepan. Bring to a low simmer on medium heat. In a hot frying pan, sauté the mushrooms quickly in the vegetable oil. Add to the soup pot. Continue to simmer for 20 minutes. Remove the sachet and season generously with sea salt. Blanch the asparagus separately and cut into 1-inch (2½ cm) pieces. Just before serving, add the asparagus and adjust the seasoning to taste.

Serves 6

Chef's note: Brown beech mushrooms, called hon shimiji in Japan, are a prized type of oyster mushroom that add a rich, nutty, mildly sweet taste. This soup has become a seasonal favourite at River Café.

Nutritional Value Per Serving (597 g): Calories 187, Protein 9.8 g, Carbohydrates 26.6 g, Dietary Fibre 8.1 g, Sugars 4 g, Total Fat 5 g, Saturated Fat 0.9 g, Cholesterol 0 mg, Sodium 47 mg

Salads

Mixed Organic Greens, Vegetable Chips and a Champagne Vinaigrette **p55** Grilled Calamari Salad **p56** Salade Auberge du Pommier **p59** Seasonal Vegetable Salad **p60** Green Tea Soba Noodle Salad with Lemongrass Prawns **p63** Grilled Calamari Salad **p64** Roasted Beets, Pickled Fennel, Spiced Pecans, Poached Pears, Blue Cheese and an Orange-Vanilla Vinaigrette **p67** Shrimp Salad with Shiitake Mushrooms, Basil and Vermicelli Noodles **p68** Tomato, Avocado and Ricotta Salata **p71** Spicy Sashimi Salad **p72** Salade Niçoise à la Bacalao **p75**

Mixed Organic Greens, Vegetable Chips and a Champagne Vinaigrette

3 heads organic baby lettuce such as arugula, red romaine, green romaine, frisée, lamb's lettuce, red oak, green oak or lolla rossa, leaves separated, washed and carefully dried

2 or 3 vegetables such as beet, parsnip, yam, blue potato, plantain, celeriac, lotus, edo, taro, sunchoke or cassava, peeled and sliced very thin

Sea salt

Champagne vinaigrette

Fleur de sel

CHAMPAGNE VINAIGRETTE:

2 tbsp (30 ml) Dijon mustard

⅓ cup (85 ml) champagne or white wine vinegar

1 tbsp (15 ml) minced shallot

1 tbsp (15 ml) minced black truffle

2 cups (500 ml) grape seed oil

½ cup (125 ml) sparkling wine

Sea salt and white pepper

CHAMPAGNE VINAIGRETTE: In a medium bowl, whisk the Dijon, vinegar, shallot and truffle together. In a slow, steady stream, add the oil, whisking constantly. Whisk in the sparkling wine and season to taste with salt and pepper.

VEGETABLE CHIPS: Working in batches, blanch the vegetable slices in boiling water for 35 seconds. Remove and roll in a cloth to dry. Deep-fry at 275°F (135°C) until just crisp. Drain on a cloth and season with sea salt.

TO ASSEMBLE: Arrange the lettuces in the bowls and spoon the vinaigrette on top. Garnish with a selection of vegetable chips and a light sprinkling of fleur de sel.

Serves 4

Chef's note: The remaining vinaigrette will stay in the refrigerator for 5 days.

Nutritional Value Per Serving (240 g): Calories 270, Protein 3.6 g, Carbohydrates 29 g, Dietary Fibre 5 g, Sugars 13 g, Total Fat 21 g, Saturated Fat 2 g, Cholesterol 0 mg, Sodium 87 mg

Grilled Calamari Salad

1 lb (450 g) U-10 calamari tubes and tentacles, cleaned

¼ cup (65 ml) olive oil

1 tsp (5 ml) chili flakes

1 tsp (5 ml) kosher salt, plus extra for various purposes

1 bunch rapini

1 garlic clove, thinly sliced

½ cup (125 ml) shaved fennel

¼ cup (65 ml) pitted black olives

2 tbsp (30 ml) capers in brine, drained

½ cup (125 ml) torn basil leaves

2 tbsp (30 ml) toasted croutons

Extra-virgin olive oil

Good-quality balsamic vinegar

Edible flowers, to garnish

With the tip of a sharp knife, lightly score the calamari tubes on the inside (the softer side). Combine 2 tbsp (30 ml) of the olive oil, chili flakes and salt in a bowl and marinate the calamari for 10 to 15 minutes. While the calamari is marinating, bring a large pot of salted water to a boil. There should be enough salt so that the water tastes like the sea. Blanch the rapini for about 3 minutes. The stems should yield when pressed between your thumb and forefinger. Remove from the pot and shock in a bowl of ice water. Drain and reserve.

In a frying pan on medium heat, sauté the garlic in the remaining olive oil until it takes on a light brown colour. Add the rapini and toss until warmed through. Season lightly with salt and remove to a cutting board. Once the rapini is cool enough to handle, cut the stalks in half and divide them evenly among the plates. Top with the shaved fennel and scatter the olives and capers over the plates.

The cooking time of the calamari will depend on their size and the heat of your grill. If the grill is hot, it should take about 2 minutes, or until the tubes roll up and are firm to the touch. Remove from the grill to a cutting board and cut the tubes into 2-inch (5 cm) rounds. Arrange the calamari on and around the rapini. Top with the basil leaves and drizzle with the olive oil and balsamic vinegar. Finish the dish with a sprinkling of croutons.

Serves 4

Nutritional Value Per Serving (183 g): Calories 198, Protein 19 g, Carbohydrates 7.5 g, Dietary Fibre 0.75 g, Sugars 0.4 g, Total Fat 9.9 g, Saturated Fat 1.4 g, Cholesterol 264 mg, Sodium 735 mg

rapini
black olives

SUGGESTED WINE PAIRING:
Villa Sandi Pinot Grigio
100% Pinot Grigio from Veneto, Italy
www.pmwine.com

Lemon

Salade
Auberge du Pommier

VINAIGRETTE:

1 good-quality anchovy filet, packed in oil

1 garlic clove, minced or crushed

A few drops olive oil

2 egg yolks

1 tbsp (15 ml) Dijon mustard

1 tsp (5 ml) grainy mustard

1 cup (250 ml) vegetable oil

1 tsp (5 ml) red wine vinegar

Juice of ½ lemon or to taste

Splash Worcestershire or to taste

Splash Tabasco or to taste

Salt and freshly ground pepper

Smash the anchovy, garlic and a bit of oil together to make a paste. In a large mixing bowl, whisk together the egg yolks, mustards and anchovy-garlic paste. Slowly add the vegetable oil, whisking constantly, to create an emulsion. Slowly add the vinegar, still whisking. Adjust the seasoning and consistency according to your taste with the lemon juice, Worcestershire, Tabasco and salt and pepper.

Serves 6

Chef's note: We serve this award-winning vinaigrette with crisp leaves of romaine lettuce garnished with braised lentils, olives and baked Parmesan crisps, with a soft-boiled quail egg on the side.

Nutritional Value Per Serving (54 g): Calories 347, Protein 1.2 g, Carbohydrates 1.5 g, Dietary Fibre 0.05 g, Sugars 0.35 g, Total Fat 39 g, Saturated Fat 5.6 g, Cholesterol 70.5 mg, Sodium 113 mg

garlic
anchovy

Seasonal Vegetable Salad

8 large Brussels sprouts

2 large heirloom carrots

2 parsnips

1 small celery root

¼ head cauliflower

¼ bunch broccoli

2 heirloom beets

1 large leek

½ cup (125 ml) good-quality Tuscan olive oil

Juice of 1 lemon

¼ bunch chives, minced

¼ bunch tarragon, minced

¼ bunch chervil, minced

¼ bunch parsley, minced

Kosher salt and freshly ground pepper

Heat oven to 400°F (200°C). Coat all the vegetables except the leek separately in a bit of the oil. Sprinkle salt and pepper on the beets and wrap in a piece of foil. Spread the vegetables on a baking sheet and add the package of beets. Cook, uncovered, until the vegetables are al dente. The beets will need to cook for about 30 minutes. When done, remove and let cool.

While the vegetables are cooking, heat the barbeque on high. Char the leek on all sides. When cool, peel and cut into bite-size pieces. When the other vegetables are cool enough to handle, peel the beets, then cut everything into bite-size pieces. In a large mixing bowl, toss the vegetables with ¼ cup (65 ml) of the olive oil, the lemon juice and the herbs. Season with salt and pepper to taste.

Serves 4

Chef's note: Add crispy bacon for a savory touch. Remember to switch up the vegetables according to what is seasonally fresh.

Nutritional Value Per Serving (339 g): Calories 385, Protein 6 g, Carbohydrates 32.6 g, Dietary Fibre 9.2 g, Sugars 11.8 g, Total Fat 28.8 g, Saturated Fat 4.1 g, Cholesterol 0 mg, Sodium 175 mg

beets cauliflower

SUGGESTED WINE PAIRING:
Pinot Gris, VQA Prince Edward County
Norman Hardie Winery www.normanhardie.com
"Very mineral driven Pinot Gris, a true expression of our calcareous limestone terroir"

Green Tea Soba Noodle Salad with Lemongrass Prawns

4 jumbo prawns, 6-8 count size, peeled and deveined

2 oz (60 g) green tea soba noodles

¼ ripe avocado, cut into ½-inch (12 mm) cubes

1 green onion, thinly sliced

Handful organic mixed greens

2 shiso leaves (Japanese mint), chopped

Sliced tomatoes, to garnish

1 tsp (5 ml) Japanese white and black sesame seeds, toasted

MARINADE:

2 tsp (10 ml) vegetable oil

2 tsp (10 ml) finely chopped lemongrass

1 tsp (5 ml) Thai fish sauce

1 tsp (5 ml) sugar

DRESSING:

3 tbsp (45 ml) unsweetened Japanese rice vinegar

2 tbsp (30 ml) vegetable oil

2 tbsp (30 ml) soy sauce

2 tsp (10 ml) sesame oil

1 tbsp (15 ml) finely chopped carrot

1 tbsp (15 ml) finely chopped red onion

2 tsp (10 ml) white Japanese sesame seeds, toasted and finely crushed

½ tsp (2 ml) finely chopped garlic

½ tsp (2 ml) finely chopped ginger

Combine the marinade ingredients, immerse the prawns and refrigerate for 2 hours. Make the salad dressing by blending all the ingredients in a blender. To cook the noodles, bring 4 cups (1 L) water to a boil. Add the noodles and cook for 8 to 10 minutes, until soft and sticky. Drain immediately and set under cold running water for about 3 minutes, until the noodles are hard and cold. Transfer to a bowl.

Heat your barbeque grill to very hot and grill the prawns for 4 to 5 minutes on each side, until pink. While the prawns are cooking, add the avocado, green onion, mixed greens and shiso leaves to the noodles and toss. Stir in three-quarters of the dressing. Place 2 prawns on each plate next to some salad and a few slices of tomato and drizzle with the rest of the dressing. Sprinkle with the toasted sesame seeds.

Serves 2

Nutritional Value Per Serving (239 g): Calories 499, Protein 10.7 g, Carbohydrates 33.6 g, Dietary Fibre 3.4 g, Sugars 5.4 g, Total Fat 39 g, Saturated Fat 5.3 g, Cholesterol 21 mg, Sodium 1827 mg

Grilled Calamari Salad

1 fennel bulb, cut into thin wedges

2 tbsp (30 ml) olive oil

Splash lemon juice

Sea salt

8 tubes calamari, left whole

6-8 tbsp (90-120 ml) canned white beans, rinsed *(see note)*

6-8 black olives, cut into quarters

6 green beans, blanched and sliced at an angle

2-3 handfuls baby arugula

CALAMARI RUB:

6-8 tbsp (90-120 ml) olive oil

1 tbsp (15 ml) paprika

1½ tsp (7 ml) ground coriander

1½ tsp (7 ml) ground fennel

½ tsp (2 ml) ground black peppercorns

6 basil leaves, finely chopped

6 mint leaves, finely chopped

Zest of 1 lemon, very fine

SPICY TOMATO VINAIGRETTE:

½ cup plus 2 tbsp (155 ml) olive oil

¼ cup plus 3 tbsp (110 ml) red wine vinegar

1 shallot, chopped

4 canned tomatoes

1 tbsp (15 ml) honey

1 tsp (5 ml) hot chili paste such as sambal or sriracha

1 tbsp (15 ml) salt

For the calamari rub, mix all the ingredients together. To make the spicy tomato vinaigrette, purée all the ingredients in a blender. This will keep 4 to 6 days in the refrigerator.

Sauté the fennel in the olive oil until lightly golden. Season with lemon juice and a little sea salt. Set aside to cool. Mix the calamari with 1 to 2 tbsp (15 to 30 ml) of the rub and let sit for 1 to 6 hours in the refrigerator. Grill or sauté the calamari for 4 to 5 minutes, turning frequently. Slice into pieces when cool enough to handle. While the calamari cooks, toss the white beans, olives, green beans and arugula with just enough vinaigrette to lightly dress the salad. Taste and add more vinaigrette if needed. Divide among the plates and top with the fennel and calamari slices. Drizzle with good-quality olive oil.

Serves 4

Chef's note: Any kind of white bean works well, whether navy beans, cannellini or borlotti.

Nutritional Value Per Serving (240 g): Calories 400, Protein 12 g, Carbohydrates 17 g, Dietary Fibre 5.5 g, Sugars 1.7 g, Total Fat 37 g, Saturated Fat 5.5 g, Cholesterol 116 mg, Sodium 6880 mg

Coriander

Vanilla

Roasted Beets, Pickled Fennel, Spiced Pecans, Poached Pears, Blue Cheese and an Orange-Vanilla Vinaigrette

2 lb (900 g) beets, assorted colours

3½ oz (100 g) good Canadian blue cheese, crumbled or cut into chunks

Alfalfa sprouts, to garnish

PICKLED FENNEL:

1 head fennel

½ cup (125 ml) water

¼ cup (65 ml) cider vinegar

¼ cup (65 ml) white wine vinegar

¼ cup (65 ml) sugar

1 tbsp (15 ml) mustard seeds

1½ tsp (7 ml) coriander seeds

½ cinnamon stick

1 garlic clove

SPICED PECANS:

1 cup (250 ml) pecans

2 tbsp (30 ml) unsalted butter, melted

1 tbsp (15 ml) sugar

1 tsp (5 ml) chili powder

Pinch cayenne

POACHED PEARS:

2 pears, peeled

2 cups (500 ml) water

1 cup (250 ml) dry white wine

½ cup (125 ml) sugar

2 pieces star anise

3 sprigs thyme

ORANGE-VANILLA VINAIGRETTE:

1 orange, zest and juice reserved

3 tbsp (45 ml) white wine vinegar

1 tsp (5 ml) Dijon mustard

1 tsp (5 ml) honey

1 vanilla bean, seeds reserved, or 1 tsp (5 ml) vanilla

¼ cup (65 ml) grape seed or canola oil

ROASTED BEETS: Heat oven to 350°F (180°C). Wrap each beet in foil and roast for about 1 hour, depending on size. The beets are done when you can insert and remove a knife easily. When cool enough to handle, remove skins with a dishtowel. Cut into desired shape and size. Set aside.

PICKLED FENNEL: Remove the fronds and stalks. Slice as thin as possible using a chef's knife or mandolin. Place in a large jar. In a medium pot, bring all the other ingredients to a simmer and cook for 5 minutes. Pour the hot liquid over the fennel and let cool. Put the lid on the jar and place in the fridge for 1 day. Can be stored in the fridge for several months.

PECANS: Heat oven to 325°F (160°C). Toss the pecans with the rest of the ingredients and place on a baking pan. Roast for about 10 minutes.

POACHED PEARS: Bring all the ingredients except the pears to just below the simmering point. Add the pears. Turn heat to low and cook about 15 minutes, until the pears are soft. Transfer to a bowl and refrigerate for 3 hours. Remove pears from liquid and cut into desired shape and size.

ORANGE-VANILLA VINAIGRETTE: In a bowl, whisk together all the ingredients except the oil. Slowly whisk in the oil to create a thick emulsion.

Serves 8

Chef's note: This salad can be tossed in a bowl and served family-style or plated up 1 ingredient at a time and served as a composed salad.

Nutritional Value Per Serving (385 g): Calories 470, Protein 7 g, Carbohydrates 41 g, Dietary Fibre 7.8 g, Sugars 41 g, Total Fat 31 g, Saturated Fat 6.4 g, Cholesterol 17 mg, Sodium 302 mg

Shrimp Salad with Shiitake Mushrooms, Basil and Vermicelli Noodles

4-6 oz (115-170 g) fresh vermicelli noodles *(see note)*

2 Roma tomatoes, blanched

¼ cup (65 ml) olive oil

12 shrimps, shells removed, deveined

10 shiitake mushrooms, dried and rehydrated, sliced

1 English cucumber, peeled and julienned

½ cup (125 ml) unsweetened coconut milk

¼ cup (65 ml) mirin

16 Thai basil leaves

1 tsp (5 ml) celery salt

½ tsp (2 ml) freshly ground pepper

To prepare the noodles, place a large spoonful in a round mould and deep-fry for about 30 seconds. Repeat 3 more times.

Cut the tomatoes in half, spoon out the seeds and crush with a fork. In a frying pan, heat the olive oil on medium and sauté the shrimp for 30 seconds on each side. Season with celery salt and pepper and set aside. In the same pan, sauté the mushrooms for 1 minute. Add the crushed tomato, cucumber, coconut milk and mirin. Cook for 3 minutes. Divide among the plates while hot and top with the fried vermicelli and shrimp. Garnish with basil leaves.

Serves 4

Chef's note: Fresh vermicelli noodles can be found at any Asian grocery store. This dish can be prepared 30 minutes prior to serving.

Nutritional Value Per Serving (258 g): Calories 376.3, Protein 10 g, Carbohydrates 37.2 g, Dietary Fibre 3.4 g, Sugars 10 g, Total Fat 21 g, Saturated Fat 7.6 g, Cholesterol 27.4 mg, Sodium 285 mg

coconut

Tomato, Avocado and Ricotta Salata

GARDE MANGER

1 large ripe tomato, cut into 8 pieces

1 avocado, cut into chunks

1 shallot, finely chopped

10 basil leaves

Olive oil croutons *(see note)*

Handful arugula

1 tsp (5 ml) white balsamic vinegar

1 tbsp (15 ml) olive oil

½ cup (125 ml) ricotta salata, grated

Maldon salt and freshly ground pepper

Place the tomato and avocado in a bowl and season with salt and pepper. Add the shallot and basil and toss in most of the croutons. Lightly crush the remaining few croutons. Add the arugula, balsamic vinegar and olive oil. Toss well. Season again with salt and pepper as necessary. Divide between the plates and sprinkle with the ricotta salata and crushed croutons.

Serves 2

Chef's note: To make the croutons, take any old bread you have in the house and cut into crouton-size pieces. Toss with olive oil and Montreal steak spice. Heat some olive oil in a frying pan and sauté the bread pieces until golden-brown, about 4 minutes. This step ensures a crispy crouton. Transfer to a baking sheet and bake at 350°F (180°C) for 10 minutes.

Nutritional Value Per Serving (305 g): Calories 516, Protein 12 g, Carbohydrates 29 g, Dietary Fibre 8.5 g, Sugars 4.8 g, Total Fat 42 g, Saturated Fat 8.4 g, Cholesterol 19 mg, Sodium 260 mg

arugula
croutons

Spicy Sashimi Salad

10 oz (290 g) fresh sushi-grade ahi tuna,
cut into 12 thin slices

10 oz (290 g) fresh king salmon, preferably
the top side, cut into 12 thin slices

6 fresh 10-20 sea scallops,
sliced horizontally into 3 rounds

10 oz (290 g) hamachi, cut into 12 thin slices

6 Japanese crabsticks, shredded into strings

7 oz (200 g) organic arugula sprouts

3 oz (85 g) daikon, peeled and sliced
on a mandolin

PONZU DRESSING:
(mix all the ingredients together):

4 tbsp (60 ml) tamari soy sauce

1 tbsp (15 ml) Sambal Oelek

1 tsp (5 ml) toasted sesame oil

Juice of 1 lime

1 tsp (5 ml) sugar

2 tbsp (30 ml) chopped cilantro

2 green onions, very thinly sliced

GARNISHES:

1 tbsp (15 ml) mixed sesame seeds

2 tbsp (30 ml) masago

6 sprigs cilantro

6 sprigs pea shoots

2 tbsp (30 ml) tropical green chili sauce

2 tbsp (30 ml) chili oil

To assemble the salad, divide the daikon among the plates, arranging it down 1 side. Top with the arugula sprouts and shredded crabstick and drizzle with 1 tbsp (15 ml) Ponzu dressing. Place the sliced fish in groups of 3 beside the salad. Garnish each plate with ½ tsp (2 ml) sesame seeds, 1 tsp (5 ml) masago, a sprig each of cilantro and pea shoots, 1 tsp (5 ml) green chili sauce and 1 tsp (5 ml) chili oil.

Chef's note: Serve this refreshing salad as a main course on a hot summer evening, or as part of a barbeque dinner or an elegant buffet.

Serves 6

Nutritional Value Per Serving (292 g): Calories 314, Protein 35 g, Carbohydrates 28 g, Dietary Fibre 1.5 g, Sugars 6.9 g, Total Fat 7.7 g, Saturated Fat 0.66 g, Cholesterol 47 mg, Sodium 1545 mg

SUGGESTED WINE PAIRING:
Sumac Ridge Estate Winery Private Reserve Gewurztraminer
One of Sumac Ridge's finest offerings and a consistent award winner.
Savour the long, zesty finish in this well balanced wine.

Cilantro

Salade Niçoise à la Bacalao

Bacalao

1 lb (450 g) boneless, skinless salt cod filets, sold in wet-packs (see note)

2-3 bay leaves

Handful peppercorns

12 mini red-skin potatoes, or any variety

4 eggs, shells washed

½ lb (225 ml) green beans
or thin asparagus, trimmed

1 head lettuce such as Bibb, red or green leaf
or mixed baby greens

2 tomatoes, cut into wedges

½ English cucumber, sliced

½ small sweet onion, thinly sliced

1 can oil-packed anchovy filets

16-20 black olives, niçoise or kalamata

VINAIGRETTE:

½ cup (125 ml) olive oil

4 tbsp (60 ml) red wine vinegar

1 tbsp (15 ml) grainy mustard

1 tsp (5 ml) honey

1 garlic clove, minced

2 sprigs parsley, minced

1 tsp (5 ml) salt

Freshly ground pepper

Soak the filets overnight. Place in a fresh pot of cold water, cover and bring to a boil. Reduce heat to medium and simmer until cooked through, about 5 minutes, and then drain. Break into bite-size pieces and set in the freezer to quick chill, or in the fridge for later use. In a pot of cold water, toss in the bay leaves and peppercorns and a pinch of salt. Add the potatoes and eggs and bring to a boil. Cook about 10 minutes. Add the green beans or asparagus and cook 3 to 4 minutes. Drain, transfer to a bowl and chill in the fridge. To make the dressing, whisk all the ingredients together except the oil. Slowly drizzle in the oil until emulsified. Taste and adjust the seasoning as necessary. Refrigerate.

When ready to serve, slice the potatoes in half. Peel the eggs and slice into quarters. Toss the lettuce with a few tablespoons of dressing and arrange among the plates. Top with the tomatoes, cucumber and onion. Lay an anchovy across each egg quarter. Sprinkle with the olives and drizzle with the dressing.

Serves 4

Chef's note: Boneless, skinless salt cod filets sold in wet-packs are usually available at grocery stores that stock Newfoundland foods, as well as at Spanish, Portuguese, Italian and Caribbean groceries. If you can't find wet-packed filets, you'll probably find very dry and hard-looking split whole fish with skin and bones intact. Don't be afraid. Simply soak the fish for several days, changing the water daily, until rehydrated, at which time they will look plumper and almost fresh, though their colour will be somewhat yellow. You'll spend more time picking over the fish for the skin and bones after boiling, but the taste is worth it.

Substitution: If garlic is too strong for your liking, a small minced shallot will give a milder taste. Guests at Bacalao love the way the briny freshness of salt cod works with the anchovies and olives, but this salad works well with pan-seared salmon or just about any type of fish.

Nutritional Value Per Serving (824 g): Calories 901, Protein 44 g, Carbohydrates 97 g, Dietary Fibre 11 g, Sugars 14 g, Total Fat 38 g, Saturated Fat 6 g, Cholesterol 244 mg, Sodium 1476 mg

Pasta & Rice

Risotto of Lobster

4 1-lb (450 g) lobsters, steamed and shelled

8 cups (2 L) lobster stock

18 oz (500 g) arborio rice

¼ cup (65 ml) olive oil

2 shallots, diced

1 onion, diced

3 garlic cloves, minced

¼ cup (65 ml) brandy or dry white wine

¼ cup (65 ml) saffron tea *(see note)*

3 tomatoes, skin and seeds removed, finely chopped

½ tsp (2 ml) minced parsley

½ tsp (2 ml) minced cilantro

Salt and freshly ground pepper

1 tsp (5 ml) butter (optional)

STOCK:

2 leeks, whites and a bit of green

2 carrots

1 onion

4 garlic cloves

2 bay leaves

3 sprigs thyme

Lobster heads and shells

To prepare the stock, simmer all the ingredients in 12 cups (3 L) water in a medium-size stockpot for about 1 hour. Discard the solids and pass the liquid through a sieve. This should leave about 8 cups (2 L) stock.

To make the risotto, heat the oil in a large stainless steel pot. On medium-low heat, sweat the shallots and onion until translucent. Add the garlic and cook a little longer. Deglaze with the brandy. Stir for 1 minute, then add the rice. Add the stock slowly, ½ cup (125 ml) at a time, stirring and making sure the liquid is absorbed before adding more.

When the risotto has been cooking for 10 minutes, add the saffron tea. As soon as the rice begins to burst out of the shell, stir in the tomato, parsley and cilantro. Season with salt and pepper. Finish by stirring in the butter. Before serving, arrange the lobster on top, sliced or cut into chunks, as you prefer.

Serves 4

Chef's note: To make saffron tea, add boiling water to a pinch of saffron and let steep. Will keep in the fridge for up to a month, or can be frozen. The risotto will cook in about 20 minutes. We like to cook our risotto past the al dente stage, which is why we use more stock.

Nutritional Value Per Serving (862 g): Calories 1140, Protein 106 g, Carbohydrates 128 g, Dietary Fibre 8.9 g, Sugars 8.9 g, Total Fat 20 g, Saturated Fat 2.7 g, Cholesterol 327 mg, Sodium 1835 mg

SUGGESTED WINE PAIRING:
Masi Masianco 2008
A modern blend of Pinot Grigio and Verduzzo
www.masi.it

Asparagus Cannelloni

Mistura

CANNELLONI:

8 sheets fresh pasta, 6 x 6 inches (15 x 15 cm)

8 slices prosciutto

8 slices asiago cheese

24 small green asparagus, peeled and blanched

8 white asparagus, peeled and blanched

1-2 tbsp (15-30 ml) butter

Extra-virgin olive oil, for drizzling

2-3 tbsp (30-45 ml) grated asiago cheese

BÉCHAMEL:

¼ cup (65 ml) butter

¼ cup (65 ml) white flour

1½ cups (375 ml) homogenized milk

1 cup (250 ml) grated asiago cheese

SAUCE:

2 cups (500 ml) vegetable stock

2 cups (500 ml) finely chopped carrots

1 tsp (5 ml) butter

1 tbsp (15 ml) olive oil

1 leek, whites finely sliced, keeping the rings intact

1 cup (250 ml) green peas, precooked

Salt and freshly ground pepper

BÉCHAMEL: In a saucepan, melt the butter over medium-low heat and add the flour. Whisking constantly, cook until the mixture takes on a golden colour. Remove from heat and let cool for 1 minute. While the flour-butter mixture is cooling, bring the milk to a boil. Return the flour-butter mixture to a low heat and add the hot milk in 5 or 6 goes, whisking vigorously and continuously to prevent lumps. The mixture will thicken quickly. Keep adding and stirring for about 20 minutes. If too thick, add more hot milk. Remove from heat and whisk in the asiago cheese until well incorporated.

SAUCE: Make while cannelloni is cooking. In a large saucepan, simmer the carrots in vegetable stock for about 10 minutes. Season with salt and pepper. When slightly cooled, place in a blender and purée until smooth. Strain to remove any larger pieces and return to pot. In a frying pan, heat butter and olive oil over medium and sauté the leeks and peas until soft. Season with salt and pepper. Scrape into the carrot stock and bring to a simmer.

TO ASSEMBLE: Heat oven to 375°F (190°C). Use a baking dish small enough for the 24 pieces of cannelloni to fit tightly together when standing on end. Prepare the dish by smearing the bottom with butter and evenly spreading about ½ cup (125 ml) of the béchamel on top. Bring a large pot of salted water to a boil. Cook the pasta sheets 1 at a time until al dente. Rinse briefly in ice water and place on a towel to dry. Divide the remaining béchamel into 8 parts. Spread the béchamel down the centre of each cooked pasta sheet. Lay a piece of prosciutto on top, followed by a slice of asiago cheese and 4 spears of asparagus. Arrange so some of the asparagus tips stick out at each end. Roll up the pasta sheets as tightly as possible. Cut each cannelloni into 3 equal parts and stand upright in the baking dish. Dot the tops with a bit of butter and cook in the oven for 20 minutes or until lightly coloured. Divide the sauce among the soup bowls and arrange 6 pieces of cannelloni in each bowl. Drizzle with olive oil and top with a sprinkle of grated asiago.

Serves 4

Nutritional Value Per Serving (746 g): Calories 1233, Protein 53 g, Carbohydrates 130 g, Dietary Fibre 12 g, Sugars 16 g, Total Fat 57 g, Saturated Fat 29.8 g, Cholesterol 158 mg, Sodium 3300 mg

SUGGESTED WINE PAIRING:
Winzer Krems Gruner Veltliner
www.eurovintage.com

Asiago

Fennel

Beet Tortellini with White Truffle Emulsion, Toasted Pine Nuts and Shaved Manchego Cheese

The Only On King

FILLING:

3 golden beets

2 shallots

2 tbsp (30 ml) olive oil

1 tsp (5 ml) fennel seeds

1 tsp (5 ml) fresh tarragon

Salt and freshly ground pepper

EMULSION:

1 cup (250 ml) vegetable stock *(see note)*

1 tbsp (15 ml) white truffle oil

1½ tsp (7 ml) lemon juice

2 tbsp (30 ml) unsalted butter

PASTA DOUGH:

2 large red beets

80 g (2¾ oz or ½ cup) durum semolina

220 g (7¾ oz or just under 1½ cups) flour

2 large eggs

1 tbsp (15 ml) extra-virgin olive oil

½ tsp (2 ml) kosher salt

1 egg yolk, for sealing tortellini

GARNISHES:

Handful arugula, tossed with a bit of olive oil and fresh lemon juice

½ cup (125 ml) pine nuts, toasted

Piece of Manchego or Parmesan, shaved

FILLING: Heat oven to 350°F (180°C). Wrap beets in foil and cook for 1 hour or until tender. Cool, peel and purée. While beets are cooking, sauté shallots in the oil until translucent. Mix into the beet purée along with the fennel seeds and tarragon. Season with salt and pepper.

PASTA DOUGH: Using a juicer, turn the red beets into juice. In a small pot on medium, reduce the juice until you have 1 tbsp (15 ml). Chill in the fridge. In a large bowl, combine the semolina, flour and salt. Incorporate the beet juice, eggs and olive oil until a ball forms. Knead for 5 minutes. The dough should keep its shape and bounce back when pressed down. Cover tightly in plastic wrap and rest in the fridge for 30 minutes. Divide into 2. Roll out each piece, then place 1 at a time through a pasta machine. Start by cutting a circle in the dough 3 inches (7½ cm) in diameter (the dough should yield about 30 circles). Dab some egg yolk along the edge of half the circle. Put 1 tbsp (15 ml) of the filling in the middle and fold into a half-moon shape. Press all around the filling to remove air pockets. Place a bit of egg yolk at the tips and pinch to close completely.

EMULSION: Can be made while the pasta dough is resting in the fridge. In a large saucepan set on medium, combine the stock, truffle oil, lemon juice and salt and pepper to taste. Heat until warm. Remove from heat and whisk in the butter. Keep warm until ready to use.

TO ASSEMBLE: Bring a large pot of salted water to a boil. Add the tortellini and cook until tender, about 3 minutes. Make sure the water simmers rather than boils rapidly so the tortellini don't fall apart. Lift out of the water with a kitchen spider and gently drop into the emulsion. Bring to a boil. Immediately remove and place in a large serving bowl. Top with the arugula. Sprinkle with the pine nuts and shaved cheese.

Serves 4

Chef's note: To make vegetable stock, simmer 1 onion, 1 carrot, 2 celery stalks and 2 garlic cloves in 8 cups (2 L) water for 1 hour, covered. Strain through a cheesecloth, return to a clean pot and reduce over medium heat by half.

Nutritional Value Per Serving (299 g): Calories 635, Protein 16.5 g, Carbohydrates 68.4 g, Dietary Fibre 6.6 g, Sugars 0.96 g, Total Fat 35 g, Saturated Fat 7.6 g, Cholesterol 161 mg, Sodium 1190 mg

SUGGESTED WINE PAIRING:
Joie Farm Rosé 2008 Okanagan Valley
Self-represented in BC and Alberta
Represented by Lifford Agency in Ontario

Stinging Nettle Gnocchi

2½ cups (625 ml) ricotta, strained overnight to remove moisture

½ cup (125 ml) blanched and chopped stinging nettle leaves *(see handling tip)*

1 large egg

1½ tsp (7 ml) kosher salt

¼ tsp (1 ml) freshly grated nutmeg

1 cup (250 ml) flour plus extra for rolling

3 tbsp (45 ml) butter

Finely grated Romano or pecorino cheese

Toasted almonds, to garnish

STINGING NETTLE: To blanch the leaves, place in boiling salted water for 30 seconds. Remove and refresh in cold water. Drain and roll in a dishtowel, squeezing out the excess moisture. Chop as finely as possible.

GNOCCHI: Combine the ricotta, chopped nettles, egg and seasonings in a large bowl and mix well. Add all the flour and with a fork or pastry cutter gently but swiftly work into a soft dough. Be cautious not to overwork as this will affect the texture of the gnocchi. Place the dough in a lightly floured bowl, cover and let rest in the refrigerator for at least 30 minutes.

On a lightly floured surface, roll the dough into 4 or 5 ropes that are ¾ inch (2 cm) in diameter. Using a small knife or pastry scraper, cut into individual pieces. Blanch the gnocchi in simmering salted water until they float, then remove and place in an ice bath to cool. When cool, drain and toss gently in oil to use later. If using right away, count 30 seconds once they float and remove to toss with the butter, cheese and toasted almonds.

Makes about 50 pieces.

Handling tip: When harvesting the stinging nettles, select young plants with bright green leaves that haven't yet flowered. Make sure to wear leather or plastic-coated gloves during the harvesting and preparation. The sting goes away once the leaves have been cooked.

Substitution: If you can't find stinging nettles, spinach works well too.

Nutritional Value Per Serving (18 g): Calories 43, Protein 2.4 g, Carbohydrates 2.9 g, Dietary Fibre 0.32 g, Sugars 0.48 g, Total Fat 2.4 g, Saturated Fat 1.4 g, Cholesterol 12 mg, Sodium 118 mg

ricotta
pecorino

Prosciutto

Risi e Bisi

2¾ cups (680 ml) chicken or vegetable bouillon

⅓ cup (85 ml) frozen peas

¼ cup plus 2 tbsp (65 plus 30 ml) butter at room temperature

½ onion, finely chopped

2 oz (60 g) thin slices prosciutto, diced

2 oz (60 g) chopped tomatoes

Pinch fennel seeds

½ cup (125 ml) Italian rice, preferably Carnaroli

1 tbsp (15 ml) grated Parmesan

Truffle oil (optional)

In a covered saucepan, bring the chicken bouillon to a boil. Meanwhile, cook the peas in boiling water, drain and set aside. In a deep-frying pan, melt ¼ cup (65 ml) of the butter and sauté the onion on medium for 2 to 3 minutes, making sure it doesn't darken. Add the prosciutto and stir over medium heat for 2 minutes. Add the peas, chopped tomatoes and fennel and stir. Incorporate the rice and stir for 2 to 3 minutes. Still on medium heat, pour in 2 ladlefuls of the hot chicken bouillon and stir slowly until absorbed. Repeat this step until the rice is tender and creamy, about 25 minutes. Remove from burner and stir in the remaining butter and Parmesan. If using truffle oil, drizzle some over each dish before serving. Makes 4 side or 2 main-course dishes.

Serves 2 to 4

Nutritional Value Per Serving (509 g): Calories 666, Protein 16 g, Carbohydrates 53 g, Dietary Fibre 2.4 g, Sugars 4.7 g, Total Fat 43 g, Saturated Fat 25 g, Cholesterol 124 mg, Sodium 3110 mg

fennel
peas

Potato Gnocchi with Tomato-Pancetta Sauce and Shaved Pecorino

TOMATO-PANCETTA SAUCE:

¼ cup (65 ml) olive oil, plus more for drizzling

¼ red onion, finely sliced

½ head garlic, finely chopped

1 tsp (5 ml) red chili flakes

Pinch chopped herbs such as savory and oregano

3 bay leaves

7 oz (200 g) pancetta, finely diced or ground

2 28-oz (840 g) cans whole tomatoes, drained, juice reserved from 1 can, crushed by hand

1 tbsp (15 ml) balsamic vinegar

Salt and freshly ground pepper

POTATO GNOCCHI:

1 lb (450 g) potatoes, peeled and diced, preferably Yukon gold

1 whole egg

¾ cup (190 ml) flour

Shavings of pecorino cheese, to garnish

SAUCE: Using a large heavy-bottomed saucepan, heat the olive oil on medium-low and sweat the onion, garlic, chili flakes, herbs and pancetta until soft, about 5 minutes. Add the crushed tomatoes and tomato juice and cook on high heat, stirring frequently, for about 15 minutes, until slightly reduced. Add the balsamic vinegar and season to taste.

GNOCCHI: Place the potatoes in a pot with a pinch of salt and bring to a boil. Reduce heat to medium and cook until just tender. Drain and return to pot on low heat. Using a wooden spoon, break up the potatoes to dry them out. After about 5 minutes they should look white and downy. Once dry, pass through a potato ricer or mesh strainer into a large bowl. Let cool before proceeding.

Add a good pinch of salt to water in a large pot and bring to a simmer. Meanwhile, add the egg to the potato purée with a pinch of salt and pepper, mixing well. Add the flour and gently knead until incorporated. Depending on the moisture content of the purée, you may need a little more flour. The dough should be soft but not sticky. Pinch off a small piece and drop into the simmering water. If the edges start to dissolve, add more flour. Repeat this step until the shape of the gnocchi holds when poaching.

Divide the dough into quarters and roll into ropes about 1 inch (2½ cm) thick. If needed, use a little flour to stop the ropes from sticking to the counter, but don't use too much because it will make them harder to roll. Cut the ropes into 1-inch (2½ cm) lengths and poach in the water for 3 to 4 minutes. Work in batches if your pot isn't large enough to prevent them from sticking to each other. When done, transfer to an ice bath for 5 to 10 minutes if reserving for later use. They should be cold all the way through. If using immediately, put straight into the tomato sauce. Finish with a drizzle of olive oil and shavings of pecorino.

Serves 4

Chef's note: An option is to fry the gnocchi in olive oil until crisp and serve on a bed of sauce.

Nutritional Value Per Serving (615 g): Calories 561, Protein 27 g, Carbohydrates 70 g, Dietary Fibre 9.4 g, Sugars 15 g, Total Fat 20 g, Saturated Fat 4 g, Cholesterol 86 mg, Sodium 2053 mg

Spring Lamb Ravioli with Morels and Fava Beans

THE Fairmont
WATERFRONT
VANCOUVER

LAMB FILLING:

1 lb (450 g) lamb shoulder

3 tbsp (45 ml) olive oil

¼ cup (65 ml) diced onion

2 tbsp (30 ml) diced celery

2 tbsp (30 ml) diced carrot

1 tsp (5 ml) chopped garlic

4 sprigs thyme

1 small sprig rosemary

10 peppercorns

2 bay leaves

1 cup (250 ml) white wine

4 cups (1 L) veal stock

1 tbsp (15 ml) butter

4 shallots, diced small

1 Yukon gold potato, cooked and passed through a sieve

¼ cup (65 ml) finely chopped parsley

PASTA DOUGH:

4 cups (1 L) flour

½ cup (125 ml) semolina

1 tbsp (15 ml) olive oil

6 extra-large eggs plus 1 for egg wash

3 egg yolks

MORELS AND FAVA BEANS:

10 tbsp (150 ml) butter

12 oz (340 g) fresh morel mushrooms, stems removed, washed

2 shallots, diced

1½ cups (375 ml) chicken stock

4 oz (115 g) fresh fava beans, peeled

Salt and freshly ground pepper

LAMB FILLING: Heat oil in a large saucepan on high and brown lamb on all sides. Remove to a plate. In the same oil still on high, sauté onion, celery, carrot, garlic, thyme, rosemary, peppercorns and bay leaves until golden-brown. Deglaze with the wine and reduce until wine is almost gone. Add stock and return lamb to pan. Cook, covered, just under the boil, for 2 to 3 hours, until tender. To avoid dryness, let cool completely in liquid. When ready to make the filling, warm lamb gently in the same liquid. Remove to a work surface. Strain the liquid and return to pot to reduce on medium until one-eighth remains. Shred the meat and place in a bowl. Melt the butter in a pan on medium and sauté the shallots. Add to lamb along with the liquid reduction, potato and parsley.

RAVIOLI: To make the dough, combine flour and semolina in bowl of a standing mixer. Add olive oil and toss until incorporated. With the mixer on slow and dough hook in place, add the 6 eggs and 3 yolks 1 at a time. Remove the dough to a floured surface and knead until smooth and supple. Wrap tightly in plastic and refrigerate for half an hour. Once chilled, roll out using the thinnest setting on the pasta machine. Drape a sheet of pasta over the ravioli moulds and place a teaspoon of filling in each mould. Brush a bit of egg wash over the seams. Place a second pasta sheet on top and roll with a rolling pin until the individual ravioli are sealed and cut. Repeat process for a total of 24 ravioli.

TO ASSEMBLE: Bring 8 cups (2 L) of salted water to a boil. Meanwhile, heat 4 tbsp (60 ml) of the butter on medium and sauté the morels for 2 minutes. Add the shallots and sauté for 1 minute. Add the stock and reduce by half, still on medium heat. Add fava beans, season with salt and pepper and reduce by half again. When water is boiling, add the ravioli, stirring carefully to prevent sticking. Cook for 4 to 5 minutes or until tender but not soft. Drain and transfer to a bowl. Toss with 2 tbsp (30 ml) of the butter and spoon onto pasta dishes. Finish the morels and favas by stirring in the remaining 4 tbsp (60 ml) of butter. Spoon sauce over the ravioli and serve immediately.

Serves 4

Chef's note: This is a wonderful dish to prepare in the spring, when all these ingredients are easy to find and at their very best.

Nutritional Value Per Serving (420 g): Calories 874, Protein 51 g, Carbohydrates 17 g, Dietary Fibre 3.4 g, Sugars 1.7 g, Total Fat 66 g, Saturated Fat 25.7 g, Cholesterol 192 mg, Sodium 526 mg

SUGGESTED WINE PAIRING:
Jackson-Triggs Proprietors' Reserve Shiraz
Canada's most awarded winery globally
Awarded Silver in the San Francisco International Wine Competition
Robust red fruit and pepper notes with a long finish

Hand-Cut Papardelle with Bacon, Shimeji Mushrooms, Ontario Cold-Pressed Canola and Canadian Feta

PASTA DOUGH:

4 whole eggs

1 egg yolk

2 tbsp (30 ml) olive oil

3 to 3½ cups (750-875 ml) flour

TOPPINGS:

½ lb (225 g) bacon, diced medium

½ lb (225 g) shimeji or other mushrooms, sliced

¼ cup (65 ml) shallots, diced

4 garlic cloves, thinly sliced

3 tbsp (45 ml) cold-pressed Ontario canola

Canadian feta, shaved

1 bunch chives, sliced

Pinch salt and freshly ground pepper

PASTA DOUGH: In a small bowl, whisk the eggs and olive oil together. In a large bowl, form the flour into a mound with a well in the centre. Pour the egg mixture into the well and, using your fingers, slowly start to incorporate the flour into the egg mixture. Continue working the flour into the dough as it begins to form. Knead for 10 minutes, until smooth. Let rest for 30 minutes. Roll out dough and cut per the instructions that came with your pasta roller. Cook pasta in a large pot of boiling, well-salted water for about 45 seconds.

TO ASSEMBLE: Render the bacon in a large frying pan over medium heat for about 6 minutes. Add the mushrooms, shallots and garlic and cook for about 2 minutes. Stir in the oil, followed by the pasta. Incorporate the feta and chives and season with salt and pepper.

Serves 6

Chef's note: This recipe is still delicious if good-quality store-bought pasta is used.

Nutritional Value Per Serving (191 g): Calories 608, Protein 24.6 g, Carbohydrates 51 g, Dietary Fibre 2.2 g, Sugars 13 g, Total Fat 33 g, Saturated Fat 8.8 g, Cholesterol 201 mg, Sodium 64 mg

shallots

Duck Confit Risotto with Seared Foie Gras

la chronique

2 tbsp (30 ml) butter, melted

1 green onion, chopped small

7 oz (200 g) arborio rice

7 tbsp (105 ml) white wine

2 cups (500 ml) duck or chicken broth *(see note)*

7 tbsp (105 ml) 35% cream

6 tbsp (90 ml) grated Parmesan plus shavings for garnish

Salt and freshly ground pepper

2 store-bought duck confit legs, shredded

1 tbsp (15 ml) olive oil

4 3-oz (85 g) slices foie gras

To make the risotto, melt the butter on medium heat and add the green onion. Cook until soft, making sure not to brown. Add the rice and cook for about 2 minutes, stirring continuously. Add the wine and stir. When it evaporates, add the stock in about 4 batches, stirring occasionally. Continue adding and stirring until the risotto is about 80 percent cooked. Keep aside a small amount of stock in case the risotto is too thick when done. Add the cream and Parmesan and cook for a few minutes before adding the duck. If necessary, add remaining stock. Season to taste. Heat the olive oil in a pan and sear the foie gras on both sides. Divide the risotto among the bowls and top with a slice of foie gras and shaved Parmesan.

Serves 4

Chef's note: To make duck broth, place duck bones, carrots, onions, celery and a bay leaf in water and bring to a boil. Season with salt and pepper. For a browner broth, place the bones in the oven first, uncovered, and cook at 450°F (230°C) for 25 minutes. The amount of liquid needed to cook the arborio rice will vary depending on the type used.

Nutritional Value Per Serving (294 g): Calories 541, Protein 24.5 g, Carbohydrates 42.3 g, Dietary Fibre 2 g, Sugars 0.5 g, Total Fat 25.4 g, Saturated Fat 13.2 g, Cholesterol 219.7 mg, Sodium 712.8 mg

SUGGESTED WINE PAIRING:
Inniskillin Reserve Pinot Noir
Vibrant strawberry and floral aromas are followed by supple tannins and delicate cranberry and plum flavours on the palate.

Butternut Squash Gnocchi

la chronique

2.2 lb (1 kg) butternut squash, halved, skin and seeds removed

1½ cups (375 ml) flour

1 egg

3 tbsp (45 ml) Parmesan

¼ tsp (1 ml) nutmeg

Salt and freshly ground pepper

Clarified butter

Garnishes: chopped chives, shavings of Parmesan

Heat oven to 400°F (200°C). Cut the squash into thin slices, place in a baking pan, cover with foil and bake for 1 hour. Transfer to a blender and blend well. Place in a strainer lined with a cloth and refrigerate for 24 hours. The next day, place 1 lb (450 g) squash in a bowl and add all the other ingredients. Mix together to form a dough. If too sticky, add more flour. Divide the dough into several pieces and roll out each piece to make a rope about 1 inch (2½ cm) in diameter. Cut each rope into 1-inch-long pieces. Place the gnocchi on a cookie sheet and freeze for later use or cook immediately. To cook, add to a pot of boiling salted water. They are ready when they rise to the top. Toss with a bit of clarified butter and sprinkle with chives and Parmesan shavings.

Serves 8

Chef's note: Gnocchi is also nice cooked in chicken stock.

Nutritional Value Per Serving (157 g): Calories 164, Protein 5 g, Carbohydrates 36.7 g, Dietary Fibre 3 g, Sugars 2.9 g, Total Fat 2 g, Saturated Fat 1 g, Cholesterol 26.6 mg, Sodium 42 mg

Fettucine all'Aragosta

2 1½-lb (680 g) lobsters, steamed and cooled

1 lb (450 g) fettucine

½ cup (125 ml) extra-virgin olive oil

½ cup (125 ml) mint leaves

½ cup (125 ml) basil leaves

1 cup (250 ml) parsley, plus chopped parsley to garnish

2 garlic cloves

4 tbsp (60 ml) salt-packed or regular capers, rinsed and drained

4 canned plum tomatoes, roughly chopped

2 tbsp (30 ml) salt

1 tbsp (15 ml) freshly ground pepper

1 tbsp (15 ml) crushed chili pepper or chili flakes

Crack the lobster shells and remove the meat. Cut the tail into ½-inch (12 mm) slices and the claws into 3 pieces each. In a blender, mix the oil, mint, basil, parsley, garlic, capers, tomatoes, salt, black pepper and chili pepper to form a smooth paste. If needed, add a little more oil. Pour into a large serving bowl.

Bring a large pot of salted water to a boil and cook the fettucine until al dente. Add the lobster to the pasta cooking water for 1 minute. Drain well. Pour the hot pasta and lobster into the bowl and toss like a salad until well mixed. Serve immediately sprinkled with chopped parsley leaves.

Serves 4

Nutritional Value Per Serving (473 g): Calories 898, Protein 54 g, Carbohydrates 99 g, Dietary Fibre 8.8 g, Sugars 7.7 g, Total Fat 31 g, Saturated Fat 4.7 g, Cholesterol 122 mg, Sodium 4592 mg

Bison Hump
and Saskatoon Berry Perogies

3 lb (1½ kg) bison hump or chuck

Salt and freshly ground pepper

2-3 tbsp (30-45 ml) vegetable oil

4 or more cups (1 L or more) bison or beef stock, enough to submerge meat

½ yellow onion, chopped

1 celery stalk, chopped

1 carrot, chopped

1 garlic clove, smashed

½ cup (125 ml) red wine

2 tbsp (30 ml) sherry vinegar

1 bay leaf

1 tsp (5 ml) peppercorns

10 juniper berries

1 sprig rosemary or a pinch dried

1 sprig thyme or a pinch dried

2 cups (500 ml) Saskatoon berries, fresh or frozen

PEROGIE DOUGH:

2 cups or more (500 ml) flour

1½ cups (375 ml) sour cream

CARAMELIZED ONIONS:

3 lb (1½ kg) yellow onions, diced very small

3 tbsp (45 ml) butter

Pinch salt

To caramelize the onion, place in a pan with the butter and salt. Cover and cook on medium-low until very tender, stirring occasionally, about 20 minutes. Uncover and continue to cook until golden-brown. The yield should be about 1 cup (250 ml).

Heat oven to 300°F (150°C). Season bison with salt and pepper. Heat oil in a frying pan on high heat and sear the hump on all sides, or sear on a grill. Place in a roasting pan and cover with stock. Add the onion, celery, carrot, garlic, wine, vinegar, bay leaf, peppercorns, juniper berries and herbs. Bring to a gentle simmer. Cover and cook in the oven for about 5 hours, until the bison is fork tender. Remove from stock, wrap tightly in plastic (braised meat dries easily if left uncovered) and let cool. Strain the braising stock and transfer to a large saucepan to reduce by three-quarters on a low boil, skimming any fat. Shred the cooked bison and add to the reduced stock with the Saskatoon berries and ½ cup (125 ml) of the caramelized onions. Heat through and season if needed. Cool completely in fridge until it becomes fairly solid.

Combine the sour cream with the flour. Mix together until dough forms, and then knead briefly. Roll out the dough and cut out about 40 3-inch (7½ cm) rounds. Place a spoonful of bison mixture on 1 side of each round and fold in half, sealing the edge by pinching the sides together. Drop the perogies into a large pot of boiling salted water a few at a time and cook until they float, plus 1 minute more. Remove from water and drain well. Quickly fry with some caramelized onion and serve with sour cream or horseradish crème fraîche, made by grating 2 tbsp (30 ml) fresh horseradish into 1 cup (250 ml) crème fraîche.

Serves 4 to 6

Chef's note: To freeze perogies, lay them on a baking sheet, not touching, and put in the freezer. Once frozen, place in a covered container for up to 2 months. Cook from frozen. Perogies are also delicious filled with a potato-onion mixture.

Substitutions: If you can't find bison, short ribs cut into 3-inch (7½ cm) pieces work very well. Instead of Saskatoon berries, you can use blueberries.

Nutritional Value Per Serving (1243 g): Calories 1172, Protein 92 g, Carbohydrates 100 g, Dietary Fibre 11.6 g, Sugars 19 g, Total Fat 39 g, Saturated Fat 20 g, Cholesterol 294 mg, Sodium 1097 mg

SUGGESTED WINE PAIRING:
Sumac Ridge Estate Winery Black Sage Vineyard Merlot
One of the most awarded vineyards in Canada.
Beautiful structure with a velvety texture follow through.

Tagliatelle con Rapini, Saisiccia e Pomodori Cilegi

Ristorante
Primo & Secondo

2 tbsp (30 ml) olive oil

1½ lb (680 g) pork sausage

1 tsp (5 ml) red chili flakes

Salt and freshly ground pepper

1 medium onion, diced

1 cup (250 ml) white wine

½ cup (125 ml) canned cherry tomatoes, with liquid

1 large head rapini, stems trimmed

5 garlic cloves, thinly sliced

18 oz (500 g) tagliatelle, fresh or dried

3 oz (85 g) Parmigiano Reggiano, for grating

In a large frying pan, heat oil over high heat. Remove the casing from the sausage and crumble the meat into the pan, making sure not to overcrowd or the meat will boil rather than fry. Add the chili flakes and salt and pepper to taste. Fry until the fat has been rendered. Remove the meat and set aside. Remove the excess fat from the pan and reduce heat to low. Add the onion and sweat until tender, making sure not to brown. Add the white wine and scrape the bottom of the pan with a wooden spoon. Add the tomatoes, raise heat to medium-high and bring the mixture to a boil. Return the sausage to the pan and cook, uncovered, still at medium-high heat, for 20 to 25 minutes. In the last 5 minutes, add the rapini.

In a large pot, bring water with 2 tbsp (30 ml) salt to a boil and add the tagliatelle. Cook until al dente, about 2 minutes for fresh pasta and 5 minutes for dried. Drain and add to the pan with the sauce. Toss over high heat for about 1 minute. Divide evenly among warm bowls and grate fresh cheese over each. Serve immediately.

Serves 4

Nutritional Value Per Serving (480 g): Calories 1294, Protein 596 g, Carbohydrates 106 g, Dietary Fibre 2 g, Sugars 3.7 g, Total Fat 66 g, Saturated Fat 24 g, Cholesterol 148 mg, Sodium 1655 mg

olive oil
pork sausage

Bacalao à la Russe

1 lb (450 g) boneless, skinless salt cod filets, sold in wet-packs *(see note)*

1 13-oz (375 g) package linguine

2 tbsp (30 ml) olive oil

2 tbsp (30 ml) butter

1 small sweet onion, finely chopped

8 oz (225 g) mushrooms, sliced

2 bell peppers, any colour, julienned

1 medium zucchini, julienned

2 garlic cloves, minced

1 tbsp (15 ml) each dill and thyme, chopped

¼ cup (65 ml) Iceberg vodka

½ cup (125 ml) 35% cream

4 oz (115 g) smoked salmon, chopped

Salt and freshly ground pepper

Garnishes: 4 slices smoked salmon twirled into rosettes, chopped dill, grated Parmesan, lemon wedges

If using filets from a wet-pack, soak overnight. In a fresh pot of cold water, bring fish to a boil and cook until just opaque, and then drain and flake. Bring a large pot of salted water to a boil and cook the linguine. Drain and reserve. While the pasta water is heating, heat the oil and butter in a large non-stick frying pan and fry onion until translucent. Add the mushrooms, peppers and zucchini and fry a few more minutes, until they begin to soften. Stir in the garlic and herbs. Deglaze with the vodka, then add the cream. Let reduce until thickened, about 5 minutes. Add the salt cod and smoked salmon and season with salt and pepper to taste. Toss the pasta with the sauce. Divide among the plates, garnish and serve.

Serves 4

Chef's note: Boneless, skinless salt cod filets sold in wet-packs are usually available at grocery stores that stock Newfoundland foods, as well as at Spanish, Portuguese, Italian and Caribbean groceries. If you can't find wet-packed filets, you'll probably find very dry and hard-looking split whole fish with skin and bones intact. Don't be afraid. Simply soak the fish for several days, changing the water daily, until the fish rehydrate, at which time they will look plumper and almost fresh, though their colour will be somewhat yellow. You'll spend more time picking over the fish for the skin and bones after boiling, but the taste is worth it. Don't use fresh cod in this recipe; the flavour won't be the same.

Nutritional Value Per Serving (525 g): Calories 793, Protein 45 g, Carbohydrates 85 g, Dietary Fibre 0.15 g, Sugars 12 g, Total Fat 27 g, Saturated Fat 12 g, Cholesterol 118 mg, Sodium 174 mg

CHEF'S CHOICE:
Iceberg Vodka

SUGGESTED WINE PAIRING:
Nine Vines Viognier 2008
Angove Family Winemakers, South Australia
Represented by Atlantic Spirits and Wines Ltd.

Vodka

Meat & Poultry

Pheasant

2 pheasants, with their livers

4 garlic cloves, minced

Pinch each thyme, tarragon, marjoram and oregano, minced

2 tsp (10 ml) crushed peppercorns

¼ cup (65 ml) olive oil, for various uses

2 large Spanish onions, chopped

Large bunch spinach, left whole

SAUCE:

3 shallots, minced

¼ cup (65 ml) butter

1 cup (250 ml) red wine

1 small garlic clove, minced

Pinch each thyme and rosemary, minced

3 cups (750 ml) veal stock or pheasant jus (made using the bones)

½ cup (125 ml) Madeira wine

Caramelized citrus *(see note)*

Salt and freshly ground pepper

SAUCE: In a medium-size saucepan on medium-low heat, sauté the shallots in most of the butter until translucent. Deglaze with the red wine. Stir in the garlic, thyme and rosemary. Add the veal stock or pheasant jus. Turn heat to medium and reduce by half. Strain through a fine sieve and return to the saucepan. Add the Madeira wine and reduce a little. Add the caramelized citrus. Reduce a bit more. Stir in the remaining butter. Season with salt and pepper.

PHEASANT: Heat oven to 350°F (180°C). Prepare the pheasants by cutting in half and removing the backbone. Rub the 4 pieces on all sides first with some of the oil, then with the 4 herbs and peppercorns. Set aside. In a small frying pan over medium heat, sauté the livers in a bit of oil until medium rare. When cool enough to handle, cut into small pieces and place in a bowl. Add more oil to the pot if necessary and sauté the onion until golden-brown. Throw in the spinach and sauté, seasoning as it cooks with salt and pepper. Add the spinach-onion mixture to the liver pieces and toss. To stuff the birds, place one-quarter of the spinach-onion mixture on top of each half bird and roll it up. Truss securely with butcher string.

Heat a 12-inch cast iron pan with a bit of oil over high heat. Sear the stuffed pheasant pieces on all sides. Reduce heat to medium and cook, turning occasionally, until all sides are golden. Place pan in the oven and roast for about 15 minutes. Let rest 5 minutes before slicing and serving.

Serves 4

Chef's note: To make the caramelized citrus, cook an equal amount of sugar and citrus rind over low heat until the mixture takes on a marmalade-like consistency. Serve the pheasant with roasted vegetables such as sweet potato, rutabaga, carrots, shallots or asparagus.

Substitution: Can use Cornish hen or poussin.

Nutritional Value Per Serving (855 g): Calories 1146, Protein 98 g, Carbohydrates 18 g, Dietary Fibre 3.3 g, Sugars 5.8 g, Total Fat 65.7 g, Saturated Fat 21 g, Cholesterol 317 mg, Sodium 826 mg

SUGGESTED WINE PAIRING:
Dan Aykroyd Signature Reserve Cabernet Sauvignon
Full and complex flavours of dark berries, plums and chocolate.
www.DanAykroydWines.com

Cornish Hen with Root Vegetables, Parmesan Gnocchi and Savoury Jus

2 jumbo Cornish hens,
halved (the butcher can do this)
2 tbsp (30 ml) extra-virgin olive oil
2 tbsp (30 ml) unsalted butter
Sea salt and white pepper
Flat leaf parsley, to garnish

GNOCCHI:
4 medium potatoes, baked, flesh removed and
rubbed through a drum sieve
¾ cup (190 ml) very finely grated Parmesan
One egg, lightly whisked
Pinch each nutmeg, salt and white pepper
1 cup (250 ml) flour

BATONS:
1-2 purple-top turnips, cut into 12 batons
1-2 carrots, cut into 12 batons
1-2 golden beets, cut into 12 batons
1 cup (250 ml) water
1 tbsp (15 ml) sugar
2 tsp (10 ml) unsalted butter
Fleur de sel

SAVOURY JUS:
4 cups (1 L) chicken stock
2 eggs, whipped and strained
¼ tsp (1 ml) toasted sesame oil

TOFU "STEAKS":
1 lb (450 g) soft tofu
Cornstarch, for dusting
1 cup (250 ml) vegetable oil, for frying

SPINACH:
2 lbs (900 g) baby spinach
2 shallots, minced
3 garlic cloves, minced
2 tbsp (30 ml) extra-virgin olive oil

GNOCCHI: Combine the potato, Parmesan, egg, seasonings and most of the flour. Knead together to form a ball. Keep adding flour until it loses its stickiness. Divide into 4 thick cylinders and cut each cylinder into 7 "pillows." Bring a large pot of salted water to a simmer and poach the pillows until they float to the top, at which point they become gnocchi. Remove to an oiled tray to cool. Cover until ready to use.

SAVOURY JUS: In a medium pot, bring the chicken stock to a boil and turn it down to a simmer. Combine the egg and oil and season lightly. Just before serving, warm the gnocchi in the stock and slowly stream in the egg-oil mixture. Remove from heat and let the egg finish cooking.

TOFU: Cut the tofu into 2-inch (5 cm) equilateral triangles. Dust each piece with cornstarch. Fry in vegetable oil heated to 350°F (180°C) until crispy. Transfer to a cloth and lightly season with sea salt.

SPINACH: Heat the oil in a frying pan on low. Sweat the shallots and garlic until soft. Add the spinach and turn it around and around until well coated with the aromatic oil. Season with salt and pepper. The spinach should cook in about 2 minutes.

CORNISH HENS: Heat oven to 400°F (200°C). Rub the 4 halves with 1 tbsp (15 ml) of the oil and season with salt and pepper. Heat the remaining oil in a large frying pan on moderate heat. Sear the hen skin-side down until golden and crispy. Add the butter and turn no more than 30 seconds to coat the halves. Transfer to a clean baking sheet, skin-side up. Finish cooking in the oven for 5 minutes, until the juice runs clear.

BATONS: These should be started in advance but finished just before serving. Their shape should be about 2 inches (5 cm) long and ¼ inch (6 mm) thick. Bring a small pot of water to a boil and blanch each vegetable separately for 45 seconds. Chill in an ice bath. Reheat all the vegetables in 1 cup (250 ml) of water with the sugar and butter. Simmer until nicely glazed, 1 to 2 minutes. Sprinkle with the fleur de sel and serve immediately.

TO ASSEMBLE: Arrange the spinach, hen, tofu and root vegetables on the plates. Add the gnocchi, egg and stock and garnish with the parsley.

Serves 4

Nutritional Value Per Serving (1183 g): Calories 1205, Protein 62 g, Carbohydrates 93 g, Dietary Fibre 16 g, Sugars 11 g, Total Fat 67 g, Saturated Fat 19 g, Cholesterol 348 mg, Sodium 1985 mg

cornish

Glazed Veal Brisket with Chestnut, Cipolline and Squash Sauté

Mistura

2 lbs (900 g) veal brisket

1 tbsp (15 ml) butter

2 tbsp (30 ml) olive oil

1 cup (250 ml) chopped onion

1 cup (250 ml) diced celery

1 cup (250 ml) diced carrot

4 garlic cloves

1 bunch rosemary

2 cups (500 ml) dry white wine

2 cups (500 ml) chicken stock

Salt and freshly ground pepper

CHESTNUT, CIPOLLINE AND SQUASH SAUTÉ:

4 1-inch (2½ cm) slices buttercup squash, peeled

2 cups (500 ml) chestnuts, peeled and blanched

2 cups (500 ml) cipolline, peeled and blanched

2 medium carrots, cut into sticks

1 fennel bulb, sliced into quarters

4 garlic cloves

2 tbsp (30 ml) butter

2 tbsp (30 ml) olive oil

VEAL BRISKET: Heat oven to 450°F (230°C). Heat 1½ tsp (7 ml) of the butter and 1 tbsp (15 ml) of the oil in a frying pan over high heat. Season the brisket with salt and pepper and sear on all sides until golden-brown. Put the vegetables, garlic and rosemary in a baking pan and place the meat on top. Spread with the remaining butter and drizzle with the remaining oil. Bake for about 15 minutes, uncovered. Turn oven down to 350°F (180°C) and cook, covered, for another 45 minutes. While the meat is cooking, keep it moist by adding the wine a bit at a time until it evaporates, then adding the stock, also a bit at a time, turning the meat occasionally. At this point the brisket should be half cooked. Uncover and start the glazing process by taking the juices from the bottom of the pan and pouring them over the meat every 5 minutes. Keep this up for a half hour or until the meat is tender. This step is tedious but worth the trouble.

CHESTNUT, CIPOLLINE AND SQUASH SAUTÉ: While the brisket is cooking, heat the butter and oil in a large saucepan on medium-low. Add the squash and sauté for a few minutes. Stir in the chestnuts, cipolline, carrots, fennel and garlic. Season with salt and pepper. Cover and cook until the vegetables are tender, stirring gently from time to time, about 10 to 15 minutes. Maintaining a medium-low heat allows the vegetables to caramelize. Adjust seasoning if necessary.

Serves 2

Chef's note: A common name for cipolline is pearl onions.

Nutritional Value Per Serving (1882 g): Calories 1729, Protein 105 g, Carbohydrates 142 g, Dietary Fibre 15.7 g, Sugars 42 g, Total Fat 65 g, Saturated Fat 20 g, Cholesterol 408 mg, Sodium 1833 mg

SUGGESTED WINE PAIRING:
2007 Santa Rita 120 Cabernet Sauvignon
Chile
Represented by Mark Anthony Brands
www.markanthony.com

Balsamico-Glazed
Lamb Ribs

Mistura

2 tbsp (30 ml) olive oil

4 lbs (1¾ kg) lamb ribs

2 onions, diced

2 carrots, diced

1 stalk celery, diced

5 garlic cloves, crushed

2 bay leaves

8 sprigs each rosemary and thyme

1 cup (250 ml) red wine

2 cups (500 ml) chicken stock

½ cup (125 ml) tomato paste

Salt and freshly ground pepper

GLAZE:

1 cup (250 ml) balsamic vinegar

⅓ cup (85 ml) maple syrup

2 tbsp (30 ml) tomato paste

RIBS: Heat oven to 350°F (180°C). Heat 1 tbsp (15 ml) of the oil in a large frying pan or casserole dish on medium-high. Season the ribs with salt and pepper and sear in batches until browned on both sides. Remove from pan and set aside. Lower heat to medium and add the remaining 1 tbsp (15 ml) oil. Sauté the onions, carrots, celery and garlic with the bay leaves, rosemary and thyme until soft and light brown, about 5 minutes. Add the wine and cook until it evaporates. Return the lamb to the pan and add the chicken stock and tomato paste. Cover and cook in the oven for 1½ hours or until the lamb is tender. Remove from pan, cover in foil and keep in a warm place until the glaze is ready. Keep the oven at 350°F (180°C).

GLAZE: Strain the liquid left over from cooking the ribs into a saucepan and discard the solids. Add the balsamic vinegar, maple syrup and tomato paste and bring to a boil. Reduce the heat and simmer, uncovered, until thick and syrupy.

TO ASSEMBLE: Brush the glaze over the cooked ribs and reheat in the oven for 10 minutes or until heated through. Cut into portions before serving.

Serves 4

Serving suggestion: These ribs are delicious garnished with thinly sliced radishes, carrots and cucumbers or drizzled with seasoned wine vinegar and mint yogurt. Another option is to add a generous dollop of tzatziki to each plate.

Nutritional Value Per Serving (867 g): Calories 1884, Protein 74 g, Carbohydrates 49 g, Dietary Fibre 3.7 g, Sugars 34 g, Total Fat 147 g, Saturated Fat 62 g, Cholesterol 336 mg, Sodium 881 mg

SUGGESTED WINE PAIRING:
Santa Alicia Carmenere Reserva
www.eurovintage.com

Balsamic

Poussin Rôti with Braised Savoy Cabbage and Apple-Juniper Broth

AUBERGE *du* POMMIER

ROAST POUSSIN:

1 poussin, about 1-3 lbs (½-1½ kg)
Salt and freshly ground pepper
1 oz (30 g) unsalted butter
1 sprig fresh thyme
2 garlic cloves, finely sliced
¼ cup (65 ml) vegetable oil, for frying
Sprigs watercress, to garnish

BRAISED SAVOY CABBAGE:

2 shallots, sliced
2 garlic cloves, sliced
½ apple, cored and sliced
2 tbsp (30 ml) unsalted butter
½ head Savoy cabbage, cored and sliced
2 oz (60 ml) apple brandy or Riesling
½ cup (125 ml) chicken stock
2 bay leaves
1 tbsp (15 ml) grainy mustard

APPLE-JUNIPER BROTH:

8 juniper berries, crushed
4 shallots, sliced
4 garlic cloves, sliced
1 apple, cored and sliced
1 tbsp (15 ml) unsalted butter
½ cup (125 ml) Calvados
2¼ cups (565 ml) chicken stock
½ bunch thyme
2 bay leaves

ROAST POUSSIN: Heat oven to 350°F (180°C). Season the bird inside and out with salt and pepper. Lift up breast skin and rub breasts with butter, thyme and garlic. Heat vegetable oil in a frying pan on medium-high. Sear the bird on all sides until golden-brown. Cook on a baking sheet in oven for 10 minutes, uncovered. When done, allow to rest for 8 minutes. Cut in half if serving 2. Flesh should be pink and juicy after resting.

BRAISED SAVOY CABBAGE: Melt 1 tbsp (15 ml) butter in a saucepan on medium-low and sweat the shallots, garlic and apples until translucent, about 15 minutes. Make sure not to brown. Stir in cabbage, then deglaze with the Calvados. Simmer, uncovered, until liquid has almost evaporated. Add chicken stock and bay leaves. Cook until reduced by half. Stir in mustard. Cover and leave on low until ready to serve. Before serving, stir in remaining butter and adjust seasoning.

APPLE-JUNIPER BROTH: Melt the butter in a saucepan on medium-low and sweat the juniper berries, shallots, garlic and apple slices until translucent. Don't let them brown. Deglaze with the Calvados and reduce by two-thirds. Add the stock and herbs and reduce by one-third. Allow 3 minutes between reductions. Taste and adjust the seasoning. Strain through a fine sieve.

TO ASSEMBLE: Warm the bowls. Spoon about ½ cup (125 ml) of the cabbage into each bowl. Place the poussin on the cabbage and add about ½ cup (125 ml) of the broth. Garnish with watercress.

Serves 1 to 2

Serving suggestion: This dish becomes a hearty meal when accompanied by boiled potatoes, heirloom broad beans, your favourite mustard and a few thick slices of crusty country-style bread.

Substitution: Cornish hen, pheasant, squab, guinea hen, capon or quail all work well in this recipe. Adjust your cooking time depending on the size of the bird.

Nutritional Value Per Serving (1640 g): Calories 1725, Protein 55 g, Carbohydrates 76 g, Dietary Fibre 17 g, Sugars 31 g, Total Fat 126 g, Saturated Fat 47 g, Cholesterol 350 mg, Sodium 3926 mg

SUGGESTED BEER PAIRING:
Iron Spike – Blonde Ale
Medium body with a sweet fruit finish,
nicely balanced by moderate, thoughtful hopping
RailwayCity Brewing Company

Fiorentina Steak with Mushroom Duxelles and Arugula with a Warm Vinaigrette

l'altro buca

1 6-oz (170 g) lean strip loin steak

8 large button mushrooms

1 shallot, peeled

1 sprig tarragon, stem removed

2 tbsp (30 ml) extra-virgin olive oil, plus extra for grilling

1 garlic clove, finely minced

2 tbsp (30 ml) balsamic vinegar

2 tbsp (30 ml) soy sauce

2 tbsp (30 ml) red wine

2 tbsp (30 ml) chicken stock

Small handful baby arugula

1 1-oz (30 g) piece Reggiano Parmesan or Grana Padano cheese, shaved

Salt and freshly ground pepper

In a food processor, combine the mushrooms, shallot and tarragon into a coarse purée. Salt lightly and place in a non-stick pan over medium heat until all the moisture has evaporated, leaving a dense mushroom paste called mushroom duxelles. For the vinaigrette, heat the olive oil in a small pot and sauté the garlic briefly, about 10 seconds. Add all the other liquids and boil until the consistency resembles a light syrup. This takes a few minutes.

Heat grill to high. Season the steak well with salt and pepper and brush with olive oil. Grill on both sides to desired doneness, then let rest for 5 minutes. Place the mushroom duxelles in a pile on a dinner plate and spread out neatly with a spoon. Slice the steak into thin pieces and fan over the duxelles. Dress the arugula with 1 tsp (5 ml) of the vinaigrette and drizzle the remaining vinaigrette over the steak. Arrange the arugula salad on top and scatter with the cheese shavings. This dish should be served warm, not hot.

Serves 1

Nutritional Value Per Serving (537 g): Calories 738, Protein 58 g, Carbohydrates 15 g, Dietary Fibre 0.37 g, Sugars 9.3 g, Total Fat 44 g, Saturated Fat 11.6 g, Cholesterol 90 mg, Sodium 3696 mg

soy sauce
tarragon
balsamic vinegar

SUGGESTED WINE PAIRING:
Rocca delle Macie "Sasyr" Sangiovese/Syrah
Tuscany, Italy
Wine Spectator's "Smart Buy"
A great example of New World-style wine made in the Old World!
Proudly represented by Saverio Schiralli Agencies

Trippa Calda alla Parmigiana
Tripe with Melted Parmesan

Ristorante
Primo & Secondo

1 lb (450 g) honeycomb tripe

¼ cup (65 ml) white vinegar

3 tbsp (45 ml) extra-virgin olive oil

2 carrots, cut into ¼-inch (6 mm) slices

1 celery stick, cut into ¼-inch (6 mm) slices

1 red onion, cut into ¼-inch (6 mm) slices

2 garlic cloves, chopped

1 cup (250 ml) canned tomatoes, crushed

4 sage leaves

Salt and freshly ground pepper

Parmigiano Reggiano

Bring vinegar and enough water to cover the tripe to a boil. Add the tripe, reduce heat and simmer for 1 hour, uncovered, or until tender and rips apart easily. Be careful not to overcook. Remove from heat and refrigerate in liquid until both tripe and liquid are very cold. Remove from liquid and slice into ½-inch (12 mm) strips.

Heat the olive oil in a frying pan until just smoking. Add the carrots, celery, onion and garlic. Sauté over medium heat until golden-brown, approximately 8 to 10 minutes. Add the tomatoes and bring to a boil. Add the tripe strips and sage leaves and season with salt and pepper to taste. Simmer, uncovered, for 15 to 20 minutes. If the mixture gets too thick, add up to 1 cup (250 ml) of the cold liquid. While still very hot, divide into warmed bowls. Grate a generous amount of Parmigiano Reggiano over each bowl to form a layer of cheese, which will melt from the heat of the dish. Serve immediately with toast or crusty bread.

Serves 6

Nutritional Value Per Serving (108 g): Calories 102, Protein 1.9 g, Carbohydrates 7.5 g, Dietary Fibre 1.9 g, Sugars 1.8 g, Total Fat 7.7 g, Saturated Fat 1.3 g, Cholesterol 1.5 mg, Sodium 102 mg

Quebec Rack of Lamb
with Warm Radicchio, Fennel and Pine Nut Salad

2 racks of Quebec lamb, trimmed

2 tbsp (30 ml) butter, melted

6 tbsp (90 ml) bread crumbs

2 sprigs rosemary, chopped

1 sprig mint, chopped

1 garlic clove, minced

Sea salt and freshly ground pepper

Chopped fresh mint, to garnish

SALAD:

1 fennel bulb, cut into 6-8 pieces

1 head radicchio, cut into 4-6 pieces

2 tbsp (30 ml) olive oil

Splash lemon juice

Sea salt

1 tbsp (15 ml) pine nuts

1 tbsp (15 ml) currants

SHERRY VINAIGRETTE:

½ cup (125 ml) olive oil

¼ cup (65 ml) sherry vinegar

¾ tsp (3½ ml) salt

½ tsp (2 ml) sugar

¼ tsp (1 ml) freshly ground pepper

Heat oven to 400°F (200°C). Rub the lamb with melted butter and coat with mixture of bread crumbs, rosemary, mint, garlic, salt and pepper. Place in a baking pan with the bones facing up and cook, uncovered, for 12 to 15 minutes for medium rare. Let rest for 6 to 8 minutes before cutting. Reserve the lamb juice for plating.

Sauté the fennel in olive oil until lightly golden. Season with lemon juice and sea salt. Add the radicchio and sauté for 3 to 4 minutes. Add another pinch of salt. Mix in the pine nuts and currants and set aside in the frying pan.

When the lamb is ready, warm the fennel-radicchio mixture. Stir in ¼ cup (65 ml) of the vinaigrette and incorporate well. Divide the mixture among the plates and top with lamb pieces. Add lamb juice and garnish. Serve with your favourite potatoes.

Serves 3 to 4

Chef's note: Remaining vinaigrette will last in the refrigerator for 5 days.

Nutritional Value Per Serving (420 g): Calories 874, Protein 51 g, Carbohydrates 17 g, Dietary Fibre 3.4 g, Sugars 1.7 g, Total Fat 66 g, Saturated Fat 25.7 g, Cholesterol 192 mg, Sodium 526 mg

radicchio
lemon juice

122

Lamb

Piglet's Belly Confit with Grilled Peppers and Fresh Cream

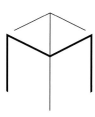

LA MONTEE

1 piglet flank

Minced thyme, to taste

Minced garlic, to taste

Coarse salt and freshly ground pepper

8 cups (2 L) duck fat

FRESH CREAM:

6 tbsp plus 2 tsp (100 ml) Mediterranean yogurt

1¼ cups (300 ml) 35% cream

Juice of ½ lemon

BBQ SAUCE:

½ cup (125 ml) raw sugar

6 tbsp plus 2 tsp (100 ml) tomato sauce

6 tbsp plus 2 tsp (100 ml) any kind of cola

GRILLED PEPPERS:

5 red peppers

4 shallots, diced

6 tbsp plus 2 tsp (100 ml) olive oil

1 tbsp plus 2 tsp (25 ml) red wine vinegar

PIGLET'S BELLY CONFIT: Prepare this the night before. Rub the piglet on all sides with thyme, garlic, salt and pepper and refrigerate, covered, for 12 hours. Heat oven to 200°F (95°C). Rinse meat and pat dry. Melt the duck fat in a large saucepan and immerse the meat. Cover and cook for at least 3 hours, until it candies. Let cool and cut into slices that weigh about 3½ oz (100 g).

FRESH CREAM: This also must be prepared the night before. Mix the yogurt, cream and lemon juice together. Cover and let sit at room temperature for 12 to 24 hours. Refrigerate.

BBQ SAUCE: To caramelize the raw sugar, place in a small saucepan on high heat and stir until melted. Add the tomato sauce and cola and reduce heat to low. Cook for about 20 minutes.

GRILLED PEPPERS: Heat grill to high. Place the peppers directly on grill and let the skin blacken. Keep turning until all sides are black. Once cool, remove the skins. Cut the peppers into slices, removing the seeds. Toss in a bowl with the shallots and a vinaigrette made from the olive oil, vinegar, salt and pepper.

TO ASSEMBLE: Divide the fresh cream among the plates. Top with the grilled peppers and the piglet confit. Spoon the sauce over everything.

Serves 8

Nutritional Value Per Serving (395 g): Calories 2151, Protein 4.4 g, Carbohydrates 20 g, Dietary Fibre 1.7 g, Sugars 15 g, Total Fat 233 g, Saturated Fat 79.8 g, Cholesterol 263 mg, Sodium 171 mg

Maple-Glazed Quail with Organic Greens and Agro Dolce Gremolata

Cafe Brio
cucina domestica

6 quails, backbone removed
and split open to lie flat

Organic salad greens for 6

Olive oil, for tossing

Salt and freshly ground pepper

MAPLE GLAZE:

1 cup (250 ml) maple syrup

½ cup plus 1 tbsp (140 ml) cider vinegar

15 peppercorns

4 sage leaves

AGRO DOLCE GREMOLATA:

⅓ cup (85 ml) raisins, soaked overnight
in cider vinegar and drained

⅓ cup (85 ml) pine nuts, toasted

3 tbsp (45 ml) coarse bread crumbs, toasted

1 tbsp (15 ml) olive oil

1 tbsp (15 ml) coarsely chopped parsley

1 tbsp (15 ml) coarsely chopped thyme

MAPLE GLAZE: Combine all the ingredients in a small saucepan and cook, uncovered, over medium heat until reduced by almost two-thirds. Strain and discard solids.

AGRO DOLCE GREMOLATA: Combine the raisins with the remaining ingredients. Season to taste with salt and pepper and toss well.

Heat grill until very hot. Brush the quails with olive oil, season with salt and pepper and place skin-side down on grill for 2 to 3 minutes, leaving the lid up. Turn over and brush generously with the maple glaze. Leave for 2 minutes longer, lid still up. Turn over again to caramelize the glaze and after 30 seconds remove from grill. Toss the greens with a bit of olive oil and salt and pepper. Divide over the serving plates and arrange the quail on top. Sprinkle generously with the gremolata.

Serves 6

Nutritional Value Per Serving (304 g): Calories 421, Protein 24 g, Carbohydrates 50 g, Dietary Fibre 3.5 g, Sugars 39.5 g, Total Fat 14 g, Saturated Fat 2.3 g, Cholesterol 64 mg, Sodium 157 mg

pine nuts
sage
thyme

quail

Duck Breast with Maple Syrup and Rose Petals

la chronique

2 14-oz (400 g) duck breasts

Pinch thyme

1 bay leaf

2 tbsp (30 ml) clarified butter

2 tbsp (30 ml) olive oil

6 tbsp (90 ml) maple syrup

6 tbsp (90 ml) dehydrated rose petals

Salt and freshly ground pepper

Bring a pot of lightly salted water to a boil and add the thyme and bay leaf. Poach the duck breasts for 2 minutes. Remove and let cool on a wire rack. Wrap and refrigerate overnight. When ready to use, season with salt and pepper.

Heat oven to 425°F (220°C). Melt the butter and oil in an ovenproof frying pan on high heat. Brown the duck for 1 minute on each side. Coat with the maple syrup and sprinkle with the rose petals. Put pan in the oven for 15 minutes, basting the duck every 3 minutes. Remove from pan, reserving the juices. Cook on a medium-hot grill for at least 5 minutes, turning once. Mix the pan juices with the broth and bring to a boil. Reduce to a simmer until sauce thickens, 5 to 10 minutes. Slice duck thinly and coat lightly with sauce. Serve with seasonal vegetables such as baby bok choy and cipollini onions.

Serves 4

Nutritional Value Per Serving (114 g): Calories 251.3, Protein 20 g, Carbohydrates 0 g, Dietary Fibre 0 g, Sugars 0 g, Total Fat 18.3 g, Saturated Fat 6.9 g, Cholesterol 97 mg, Sodium 57 mg

SUGGESTED WINE PAIRING:
Le Clos Jordanne Village Reserve Pinot Noir
Red berries and a long mineral finish
Available at www.leclosjordanne.com

Braised Short Ribs on
Garlic Mashed Potatoes with
Fiddleheads and Yellow Beets

BRAISED SHORT RIBS:

3 large onions, roughly chopped

4 large carrots, chopped
into 2-inch (5 cm) chunks

3-4 celery stalks, roughly chopped

3 garlic heads, cut in half

2 sprigs each rosemary and thyme

1 star anise

1 cinnamon stick

6 beef short ribs, trimmed of outer fat

Coarse salt and freshly ground pepper

1 cup (250 ml) flour

2 tbsp (30 ml) canola oil

2 3-cup (750 ml) bottles red wine

2 tbsp (30 ml) cocoa powder

1 cup (250 ml) brown sugar

1 tbsp (15 ml) butter

GARLIC MASHED POTATOES:

1 garlic head, top sliced off

1 tbsp (15 ml) good fruity olive oil

Sprig or 2 fresh herbs such as rosemary or thyme

6 large Yukon Gold potatoes, scrubbed but
not peeled, cut in half

⅓-½ cup (75-125 ml) butter

1 cup (250 ml) 35% cream

FIDDLEHEADS AND YELLOW BEETS:

12 baby yellow beets

5 handfuls fiddleheads, well rinsed

2 tbsp (30 ml) butter

1 large shallot, finely julienned

BRAISED SHORT RIBS: Heat oven to 350°F (180°C). Place the onion, carrot, celery, garlic, herbs and spices in a large bowl. Season ribs well with salt and dredge in flour until coated. In a wide soup pot, heat oil on high. Sear ribs until browned, about 3 minutes per side. Remove from pot and set aside. Transfer the vegetables to the same pot, still on high heat. Stirring to pick up the brown bits, cook until caramelized. Add the ribs back to the pot and pour in the wine. Ensure the ingredients are covered. If not, top up with water. Add the cocoa powder and brown sugar and bring to a boil. Place in the oven, covered, until fork tender, about 3 hours. Remove ribs to a platter and strain the cooking liquid. Save the solids for another use or discard. Boil the cooking liquid in a wide shallow pan until reduced by half. Add butter at the end for sheen and flavour.

GARLIC MASHED POTATOES: Heat oven to 350°F (180°C). Drizzle garlic head with olive oil and sprinkle generously with salt and pepper. Wrap in foil along with the herbs. Roast for 1 hour. While roasting, fill a large pot with water and add a few pinches salt. Add the potatoes and bring to a boil. Reduce heat and simmer until fork tender. Do not overcook or potatoes will be soggy. Drain off the water, leaving potatoes in the pot. Add the butter and cream and mash well. Squeeze the roasted garlic into the potatoes and stir until incorporated. Season with salt and pepper. The consistency should be a little lumpy.

FIDDLEHEADS AND YELLOW BEETS: Boil the beets, skin on, in a pot of salted water for about 25 minutes, until fork tender. Using a cloth, peel while still hot. Slice into wedges. In a large frying pan on medium-low heat, sauté the fiddleheads in the butter along with the shallots. Season to taste with salt and pepper. Stir in the beets and adjust seasoning as necessary.

Serves 4 to 6

Nutritional Value Per Serving (1425 g): Calories 1702, Protein 44 g, Carbohydrates 206 g, Dietary Fibre 22 g, Sugars 62 g, Total Fat 68 g, Saturated Fat 34 g, Cholesterol 204 mg, Sodium 606 mg

SUGGESTED BEER PAIRING:
Sleeman Honey Brown
A full-bodied lager with a touch of natural honey
and a slightly sweet finish
Sleeman Breweries Ltd.

Potato Gnocchi with Shredded Pork, Roasted Pearl Onions and Spaghetti Squash

Catch
RESTAURANT & OYSTER BAR

1 lb (450 g) pork shoulder
4 tbsp (60 ml) ground anise
1 tbsp (15 ml) cinnamon
Salt and freshly ground pepper
2 tbsp (30 ml) olive oil
¼ cup (65 ml) chicken stock
1 tbsp (15 ml) butter
Several sprigs thyme, leaves only

POTATO GNOCCHI:
2 large russet potatoes
1-2 cups (250-500 ml) flour *(see note)*
2 eggs
3 sprigs thyme, leaves only
1-2 tbsp (15-30 ml) olive oil

ROASTED PEARL ONIONS:
12 pearl onions, peeled and quartered
¼ cup (65 ml) olive oil

ROASTED SPAGHETTI SQUASH:
1 spaghetti squash
1 tbsp (15 ml) butter, softened
Pinch nutmeg

CASSIS-BROWN BUTTER SAUCE:
2 cups (500 ml) cassis juice *(see note)*
2 oz (60 g) red beets, peeled and finely diced
1 cinnamon stick
1 sprig thyme
1 tbsp (15 ml) butter

ROASTED PORK: Heat oven to 450°F (230°C). Combine anise, cinnamon, salt and pepper and rub into pork. Marinate for 30 minutes in refrigerator. Place pork in a large pan and roast, uncovered, for 15 minutes. Turn heat to 350°F (180°C). Still uncovered, roast until internal temperature reads 329°F (165°C), 45 minutes to 1 hour. If getting too brown, cover with foil. When cooled, shred into small pieces.

ROASTED PEARL ONIONS: These are roasted at 350°F (180°C) and can be put in the oven with the pork. Toss the onion pieces with olive oil and salt and pepper to taste. Roast on a baking pan until tender, about 5 minutes.

ROASTED SPAGHETTI SQUASH: Also roast at 350°F (180°C). Can be put in the oven with the pork and onions. Cut squash in half and remove seeds. Rub inside with butter, nutmeg, thyme and salt and pepper to taste. Place flesh-side down in a baking pan and add water to reach ½ inch (12 mm) up the sides of pan. Bake, uncovered, for 30 minutes. Cool slightly and remove flesh with a fork.

CASSIS-BROWN BUTTER SAUCE: Mix the cassis juice, beets, cinnamon and thyme in a saucepan. Place over medium-low heat and reduce until thick and dark, 15 to 30 minutes. Strain into a saucepan and discard the solids. While the mixture is reducing, place the butter in a pan over medium heat for about 30 seconds, until the milk solids turn brown and the butter gives off a nutty aroma. Add to the reduction.

POTATO GNOCCHI: If your oven is big enough, the potatoes can roast at the same time as the pork and vegetables until fork tender. When cool enough to handle, peel and pass through a potato ricer. Combine riced potatoes with the flour, thyme and salt and pepper to taste. Add eggs. Mix together gently; be careful not to knead too much or it will become hard. Roll into long ropes about the thickness of your middle finger. Cut into 1-inch (2½ cm) pieces. Place gnocchi in a pot of boiling salted water and cook until they float to the top. Drain and toss in a small amount of oil.

TO ASSEMBLE: Heat the cassis-brown butter sauce on medium-low. Place a large saucepan over medium heat and add the olive oil. Toss in the shredded pork, pearl onions and spaghetti squash and heat through. Add the gnocchi and continue heating. Stir in the chicken stock and butter. Season with thyme and salt and pepper. Remove from heat and distribute evenly over plates. Decorate with the cassis-brown butter sauce.

Serves 4

Chef's note: How much flour you use when making the gnocchi depends on the moisture content of the potatoes. Start with 1 cup (250 ml) and add more as needed. Cassis juice can be found at most good supermarkets and health food stores.

Substitution: Instead of pork, try chicken thighs and legs.

Nutritional Value Per Serving (510 g): Calories 813, Protein 38 g, Carbohydrates 61 g, Dietary Fibre 6 g, Sugars 3.3 g, Total Fat 47 g, Saturated Fat 14 g, Cholesterol 176 mg, Sodium 250 mg

SUGGESTED WINE PAIRING:
Pascual Toso Merlot
www.eurovintage.com

Ginger-Soy Marinated and Seared Alberta Beef

12 oz (340 g) Alberta beef
tenderloin or sirloin

2-3 tbsp (30-45 ml) olive oil

MARINADE:

¼ cup (65 ml) mirin

2 tbsp (30 ml) sesame oil

2 tbsp (30 ml) soy sauce

1 tbsp (15 ml) sake

1 tbsp (15 ml) unsweetened rice wine vinegar

½ tbsp (7 ml) ginger juice *(see note)*

CITRUS SOY SAUCE:

1 shallot, finely chopped

1 tomato, finely chopped

2 tbsp (30 ml) soy sauce

Juice of 2 lemons

Juice of 1 lime

1 tbsp (15 ml) bonito flakes, finely ground

Honey to taste

RADISH AND CARROT SALAD:

¼ cup (65 ml) julienned radishes

¼ cup (65 ml) julienned carrots

¼ cup (65 ml) julienned cucumbers

2 tbsp (30 ml) finely chopped ginger

1 tsp (5 ml) sesame oil

Salt and freshly ground pepper

Combine the marinade ingredients in a freezer bag and add the beef. Marinate in the refrigerator for 3 to 6 hours. While the beef is marinating, make the citrus soy sauce by combining all the ingredients. Just before cooking the beef, toss together the ingredients for the radish and carrot salad.

Heat a heavy-bottomed pan on high. When pan is hot, add enough oil to cover the bottom. Cook beef on first side for 1 to 2 minutes, until golden-brown. Roll over and cook another minute. Continue cooking on all sides, 30 seconds to 1 minute per side. Remove from heat and leave in pan for a few minutes to continue warming the interior of the meat. Cut into ¼-inch (6 mm) slices just before serving. Place a small amount of salad in the centre of each plate. Arrange 4 to 6 slices of beef on top and drizzle the citrus soy sauce around the plate. Garnish with black and white sesame seeds and finely chopped ginger or chives and serve.

Serves 4

Chef's note: To make ginger juice, grate about 1 inch (2½ cm) ginger and squeeze to release the juices.

Nutritional Value Per Serving (242 g): Calories 404, Protein 26 g, Carbohydrates 15 g, Dietary Fibre 0.14 g, Sugars 10.3 g, Total Fat 25 g, Saturated Fat 5.8 g, Cholesterol 72 mg, Sodium 1377 mg

sesame oil
cucumber

SUGGESTED WINE PAIRING:
Jackson-Triggs
Proprietors' Grand Reserve Merlot
Intense deep red in colour with hints of black cherry and plum

Cumin

Moose Tourtière with Partridgeberry Mustard

PASTRY:

2¼ cups (565 ml) flour

1 tsp (5 ml) salt

½ cup (125 ml) cold butter, cut into ½-inch (12 mm) cubes

½ cup (125 ml) cold margarine, cut into ½-inch (12 mm) cubes

3-4 tbsp (45-60 ml) ice water

FILLING:

2-3 tbsp (30-45 ml) olive oil

1-2 tbsp (15-30 ml) butter

1 onion, finely chopped

1 lb (450 g) ground moose

2 garlic cloves, chopped

3 sprigs thyme or 1 tsp (5 ml) dried

1 tsp (5 ml) chopped rosemary or ½ tsp (2 ml) dried

¼ tsp (1 ml) each ground allspice, cloves and dry mustard

Salt and freshly ground pepper

1 tbsp (15 ml) flour

3-4 tbsp (45-60 ml) red wine or water

1 medium potato, boiled and mashed

PARTRIDGEBERRY MUSTARD:

½ cup (125 ml) partridgeberry or dry white wine

¼ cup (65 ml) mustard seeds

2 tbsp (30 ml) wine vinegar

2 tsp (10 ml) ground mustard

½ tsp (2 ml) salt

¼ tsp (1 ml) each allspice, cinnamon, garlic powder, cumin and ground coriander

Pinch each cloves and freshly ground pepper

½ cup (125 ml) partridgeberries

4 tbsp (60 ml) sugar

PARTRIDGEBERRY MUSTARD: Start 2 days before. Soak the mustard seeds in the wine overnight. In a food processor, blend with vinegar, mustard, salt and spices for 1 to 2 minutes, until a coarse paste forms. Bring the partridgeberries, sugar and 2 tbsp (30 ml) water to a boil, then reduce heat and simmer until mixture has a jam-like consistency. Add mustard-spice mixture and simmer, stirring, until thickened, 5 to 10 minutes. If too thick, add wine or water. You should have about 1½ cups (375 ml). Adjust with sugar, vinegar, salt or pepper to taste. Refrigerate overnight or up to 1 month. At first it is spicy, but after a few days in the fridge the flavours mellow.

PASTRY: In a food processor, whiz together the flour and salt. Add the butter and margarine and pulse a few times. Slowly add the ice water. Keep pulsing until the pastry comes together in a shaggy ball. Use more or less water as necessary. Do not overprocess. Remove dough, pat into a ball and cut in half. On a lightly floured board, roll out dough into a circle about 1 inch (2½ cm) larger than your 9-inch (23 cm) pie plate. Fit the pastry into the pie plate, letting the extra hang over. Chill in fridge while you roll out the top to about the same size. Lay on a plastic-lined baking sheet and chill in fridge.

FILLING: In a large frying pan on medium-high, add 2 tbsp (30 ml) oil and 1 tbsp (15 ml) butter and fry the onion until soft. Add the moose and fry, breaking it up, until three-quarters cooked, adding more oil or butter as needed. Stir in the garlic, herbs and spices and fry a few more minutes. Add the flour and fry, stirring, until browned, 1 to 2 minutes. Deglaze the pan with the wine. When the liquid has nearly evaporated, remove from heat and add the potato. Transfer to a bowl and let cool for 10 to 15 minutes.

TO ASSEMBLE: Heat oven to 350°F (180°C). Let the pastry warm on the counter for 5 to 10 minutes, until pliable. Pack the filling into the pie crust and drape with the pastry top. Press the edges together and tuck under. Flute with your thumb and forefinger or press with a fork. Make 2 or 3 short slices in the top crust to allow steam to escape. Bake for about 30 minutes, until crust is golden.

Serves 6

Chef's note: The berries Newfoundlanders call partridgeberries are known as lingonberries in Scandinavia. They resemble cranberries but are smaller and more intensely flavoured. A grocery store that stocks ingredients from Newfoundland may have them frozen or prepared as a jam. Otherwise, try European markets or Scandinavian specialty stores. If you can only find jam, skip the step of simmering the berries with the sugar and water and add 3 tbsp (45 ml) jam to the simmering mustard mixture.

Substitution: If moose is unavailable, use ground venison, caribou, boar, buffalo or other wild game. If you can't find partridgeberries, use cranberries, but add a tiny pinch of ground coriander or bay leaf to the recipe.

Nutritional Value Per Serving (282 g), Calories 682, Protein 24 g, Carbohydrates 54 g, Dietary Fibre 36 g, Sugars 8.3 g, Total Fat 39 g, Saturated Fat 15 g, Cholesterol 90 mg, Sodium 165 mg

Saltimbocca alla Romana

4 5-oz (150 g) veal cutlets, thinly sliced

4 thin slices prosciutto

8 sage leaves

1 cup (250 ml) flour, for dredging

Kosher salt and freshly ground pepper

2 tbsp (30 ml) extra-virgin olive oil

2 tbsp (30 ml) unsalted butter

2 tbsp (30 ml) dry white wine or port

¼ cup (65 ml) chicken broth or demi-glace

Garnish: rosemary sprigs, lemon wedges

Put the veal cutlets side by side on a sheet of plastic wrap. Lay a slice of prosciutto on top of each cutlet plus 2 sage leaves and cover with another piece of plastic. Gently flatten the cutlets with a rolling pin or meat mallet until about ¼-inch (6 mm) thick and the prosciutto and sage have adhered to the veal. Put some flour in a shallow platter and season with a fair amount of salt and pepper, mixing with a fork to combine. Dredge the veal in the flour, shaking off the excess.

Heat the oil and 1 tbsp (15 ml) butter in a large frying pan over medium heat. Working in batches, put the veal in the pan prosciutto-side down. Cook for 3 minutes, until crisp, and then flip over. Sauté the other side for 2 minutes or until golden. Transfer to a serving platter and keep warm. Still on medium heat, add the wine to the pan, stirring to loosen any bits from the bottom. Cook for a minute to burn off some of the alcohol. Add the chicken broth and remaining 1 tbsp (15 ml) butter. Season with salt and pepper and let reduce for 1 minute. Pour the sauce over the saltimbocca, garnish with rosemary sprigs and lemon wedges and serve immediately.

Serves 4

Suggested side dish: Roasted vegetables and potatoes.

Nutritional Value Per Serving (158 g): Calories 487, Protein 31 g, Carbohydrates 25 g, Dietary Fibre 0.96 g, Sugars 0.16 g, Total Fat 28 g, Saturated Fat 10.4 g, Cholesterol 118 mg, Sodium 557 mg

SUGGESTED WINE PAIRING:
Max Reserva Cabernet Sauvignon
Wine of Chile
Represented by Philippe Dandurand Wines Ltd.

Fish

Chive Jus

Red Snapper and Green Bean Salad in Chive Jus

4 7-oz (200 g) red snapper filets, skin on
¼ cup (65 ml) extra-virgin olive oil
Sea salt
1 lemon, cut in half
Fleur de sel
Chive jus
1 small carrot, minced
1 purple top turnip, minced
2 blue potatoes, minced
1 red bell pepper, minced
1 yellow bell pepper, minced
1 zucchini, minced
½ bunch chives, minced

GREEN BEAN SALAD:
6 tbsp (90 ml) extra-virgin olive oil
Two shallots, minced
12 oz (340 g) French green beans, blanched
and cut into ½-inch (12 mm) lengths
2 Roma tomatoes, cut into small cubes
1 tbsp (15 ml) apple cider vinegar
2 tbsp (30 ml) julienned flat leaf parsley
Freshly cracked pepper
Sea salt
Parsley oil, to garnish (optional)

CHIVE JUS:
2 cups (500 ml) chicken stock
3 green onions, whites only, roughly chopped
2 leeks, whites only, roughly chopped
1 bunch chives, roughly chopped
1 tsp (5 ml) low-sodium soy sauce
10 pink peppercorns

CHIVE JUS: Place ingredients in a pot. Bring to a boil and turn heat to low. Simmer, lid on, for 10 minutes. Turn heat off and let sit for 10 minutes. Pour through a fine sieve and discard solids.

GREEN BEAN SALAD: Warm a frying pan on medium-low and add 5 tbsp (75 ml) of the oil. Stir in the shallots. Cook for a few minutes, making sure not to brown. Add the precooked beans and toss. Add the tomato, vinegar and parsley and season to taste. Drizzle in the remaining olive oil.

SNAPPER: Ask your fishmonger to filet the fish and remove the pin bones. Heat oven to 350°F (180°C). Place a large non-stick pan on medium-high heat and pour in enough oil to coat the pan. Season the filets on both sides with the sea salt. Sear for 1 minute on each side. Transfer to a sheet pan and finish in the oven until cooked, about 7 minutes. Squeeze both lemon halves over the fish and add any remaining olive oil. Sprinkle lightly with fleur de sel.

TO ASSEMBLE: Bring the chive jus to a boil and add the carrots, turnips, potatoes, peppers, zucchini and chives. Divide the bean salad among the plates and arrange the fish on top. Spoon the chive jus around each plate and serve at once.

Serves 4

Substitution: Bass or sea bream also work well in this recipe. Any vegetables may be used for the chive jus.

Nutritional Value Per Serving (690 g): Calories 751, Protein 85 g, Carbohydrates 58 g, Dietary Fibre 16 g, Sugars 8 g, Total Fat 30 g,
Saturated Fat 4.8 g, Cholesterol 76 mg, Sodium 1185 mg

Arctic Char in Tomato Water with a Fine Herb Mayonnaise

Scaramouche

2 lbs (900 g) Arctic char filets, pin bones removed and skin left on

TOMATO WATER:

2 lbs (900 g) ripe tomatoes

1 tbsp (15 ml) salt

FINE HERB MAYONNAISE:

2 tbsp (30 ml) fresh lemon juice

1 large shallot, finely diced

1½ tsp (7 ml) Dijon mustard

1 egg yolk

1 cup (250 ml) extra-virgin olive oil

2 tbsp (30 ml) chopped chervil

1 tbsp (15 ml) snipped chives plus extra to garnish

1½ tsp (7 ml) chopped parsley

1½ tsp (7 ml) chopped tarragon

Salt and freshly ground pepper

AROMATIC WATER:

8 cups (2 L) water

⅔ cup (150 ml) white wine vinegar

3 oz (85 g) carrot, thinly sliced

3 oz (85 g) onion, thinly sliced

3 oz (85 g) leek, thinly sliced

2 tbsp (30 ml) black peppercorns

1 tbsp (15 ml) kosher salt

1 bay leaf

6 sprigs each parsley and thyme

TOMATO WATER: Purée the tomatoes in a food processor, leaving 1 aside to mince for garnish. Place in a bowl, add the salt and mix well. Drape a clean, lint-free cloth over another bowl and tip the tomatoes onto the cloth. Gather up the corners and tie with string to make a secure bundle. Suspend the bundle over the bowl in your refrigerator or other cool place for 24 hours. Strain the liquid through a coffee filter and chill in the fridge.

FINE HERB MAYONNAISE: Place the lemon juice in a mixing bowl. Add the shallots, mustard, salt and pepper. Whisk in the yolk. Whisking steadily, slowly pour in the olive oil to form a thick emulsion. Correct the seasoning. Stir in half the herbs now and the remainder just prior to serving.

AROMATIC WATER: Combine all of the ingredients and bring to a boil. Reduce heat and let simmer for 20 minutes, uncovered. Remove from heat if not using immediately.

TO ASSEMBLE: Bring the fish to room temperature to ensure even cooking. Heat the aromatic water to a simmer. Season the fish with salt and pepper. Slip it into the water skin-side up and let cook until slightly pink on the inside. Remove and place on a cutting board skin-side up. Peel the skin away by pulling carefully from one end to the other. It should come off in 1 motion. Sprinkle with a little salt and slice into portions. Place each portion in a serving bowl and pour in some tomato water. Put about 1 tbsp (15 ml) of the mayonnaise on top and garnish with a few light greens. Add the minced tomato and chive to the water. Serve immediately while the fish is still warm and the tomato water is chilled.

Serves 4 to 6

Chef's note: You will use only a portion of the mayonnaise. Keep in the fridge for another use.

Nutritional Value Per Serving (534 g): Calories 456, Protein 62 g, Carbohydrates 18 g, Dietary Fibre 3.8 g, Sugars 6.2 g, Total Fat 20.21 g, Saturated Fat 3.15 g, Cholesterol 121 mg, Sodium 1963 mg

Seared Rare Bigeye Tuna with Green Papaya Salad

nota bene

4 4-oz (115 g) bigeye tuna steaks

2 tbsp (30 ml) vegetable oil

1 cup (250 ml) thinly sliced green papaya

½ cup (125 ml) thinly sliced daikon

½ cup (125 ml) thinly sliced English cucumber

1 Anaheim chili, thinly sliced into rounds

1 lime leaf, finely sliced

¼ cup (65 ml) torn mint leaves

¼ cup (65 ml) torn Thai basil leaves

¼ cup (65 ml) roasted cashews

1 tsp (5 ml) sumac

½ cup (125 ml) chopped cilantro, stems reserved

½ cup (125 ml) Thai vinaigrette

Salt and coarsely ground pepper

THAI VINAIGRETTE:

½ cup (125 ml) chopped cilantro stems

3 bird's-eye chilis (see note)

½ garlic clove

½ lemongrass stalk

2 tbsp (30 ml) palm sugar

½ cup (125 ml) fresh lime juice

¼ cup (65 ml) fish sauce

1 tsp (5 ml) sugar

THAI VINAIGRETTE: Combine the ingredients in a blender. If necessary, adjust the seasoning with the fish sauce (to add salt) and white sugar (to add sweetness). This recipe makes about 2 cups (500 ml), but only 2 tbsp (30 ml) are needed per serving.

SEARED TUNA: Heat a cast iron frying pan until smoking hot. While pan is heating, season tuna steaks with salt and pepper, then rub liberally with vegetable oil. Sear for 10 seconds per side, turning each steak 90 degrees until all sides are seared. Remove to a cutting board and let rest 1 minute. Combine the papaya, daikon, cucumber, Anaheim chili, lime leaf, mint and Thai basil in a bowl. Dress lightly with the vinaigrette. Divide the salad evenly among the plates. Slice the tuna across the grain into 1-inch (2½ cm) slices. Arrange on top of the salad. Sprinkle the plate with the cashews and sumac and top with the cilantro leaves and a drizzle of the vinaigrette.

Serves 4

Chef's note: A Japanese mandolin with a julienne blade attachment will make preparing this salad much easier. Bird's-eye chilis are small and red.

Nutritional Value Per Serving (190 g): Calories 193, Protein 28.8 g, Carbohydrates 7.4 g, Dietary Fibre 1.2 g, Sugars 2.9 g, Total Fat 5.3 g, Saturated Fat 0.98 g, Cholesterol 51 mg, Sodium 115 mg

cilantro lime juice

SUGGESTED WINE PAIRING:
Anselmi San Vincenzo
A blend of Garganega and Chardonnay from Veneto, Italy
www.pmwine.com

Halibut Basquaise

PIED-À-TERRE

1 halibut filet, about 4½ oz (125 g)

Salt and ground espelette pepper

2½ tbsp (37 ml) extra-virgin olive oil

1 oz (30 g) dry chorizo sausage,
cut into thin rings

½ small onion, diced small

¼ cup (65 ml) red pepper, diced small

¼ cup (65 ml) yellow pepper, diced small

¼ cup (65 ml) zucchini, diced small

1 garlic clove, very thinly sliced

4 large mussels in shell, scrubbed

1 tomato, peeled and seeded,
or 4 cherry tomatoes, halved

3½ tbsp (52 ml) dry sherry

1 tbsp (15 ml) sherry vinegar

1 fresh bay leaf

Heat oven to 425°F (220°C). Season the halibut to taste with salt and espelette pepper, then drizzle with half the olive oil and place on a piece of parchment paper on a small cookie sheet. Bake for about 8 minutes. In a small pot with a tight-fitting lid, heat the remaining olive oil on medium and add the sausage, onion, red and yellow pepper, zucchini and garlic. Cook for 1 minute. Add the mussels, tomato, sherry and sherry vinegar and bay leaf. Stir to combine. Cover the pot, turn up the heat to medium-high and steam until the mussels open, about 2 minutes. Discard mussels that don't open. Arrange the mussels in their shells in a soup bowl, spoon the sausage and pepper broth into the middle and place the halibut on top. Serve with a green salad and crusty bread.

Serves 1

Nutritional Value Per Serving (532 g): Calories 776, Protein 45 g, Carbohydrates 17 g, Dietary Fibre 2.9 g, Sugars 6.2 g, Total Fat 54 g, Saturated Fat 10.4 g, Cholesterol 89 mg, Sodium 972 mg

SUGGESTED WINE PAIRING:
Chat en Oeuf "Rosé" Lanquedoc-Roussillon
Southern France
2009 winner of the *Wine Access* international wine competition "Top Rosé."
Proudly represented by Saverio Schiralli Agencies

148

Rainbow Trout with Yellowfoot Chanterelles and Crab-Stuffed Butter Lettuce

blue water cafe

4 small or 2 large rainbow trout

1 small yellow-flesh potato, peeled and diced

6 tbsp (90 ml) butter

¼ cup (65 ml) 18% cream

Pinch nutmeg

2 firm heads butter lettuce

4 tbsp (60 ml) olive oil

2 shallots, finely diced

1 sprig thyme

1 cup (250 ml) good vermouth

6 oz (170 g) fresh Dungeness crabmeat, picked through to remove any small shells

1 tbsp (15 ml) mayonnaise

½ lemon

1 tbsp (15 ml) Dijon mustard

1 tbsp (15 ml) chopped tarragon

1 shallot, finely diced

1 garlic clove, finely chopped

8 oz (225 g) yellowfoot chanterelle mushrooms, whole if small, cut in half if large

1 tbsp (15 ml) chopped parsley

Salt and freshly ground pepper

Cut the filets off the trout and remove pin bones. Cut in half and season with salt and pepper. Cover and reserve in fridge until ready to use. Cook potatoes in boiling salted water until soft. Drain and mash with the cream and 1 tbsp (15 ml) of the butter. Pass through a fine-mesh strainer and season with salt and nutmeg. Remove the dark outer leaves of the lettuce and discard. Cut the 2 yellow centres in half and season with salt and pepper. Heat a large frying pan on medium and add 1 tbsp (15 ml) olive oil. Sweat the shallots and thyme for 2 minutes and deglaze with the vermouth. Add the lettuce halves, cover and cook for 4 minutes, or until wilted. Place on a plate, pressing down to remove excess liquid. Reserve the liquid for the sauce. Cut off the bases of the lettuce halves and chop roughly. Mix bases with crabmeat, mayonnaise and a squeeze of lemon juice. Divide into quarters and form rolls 3 inches (7½ cm) long. Place a roll on each of the cooked lettuce halves and roll to form long cylinders.

TARRAGON-MUSTARD SAUCE: Pour the liquid from the lettuce into a small saucepan and bring to a simmer. Add 4 tbsp (60 ml) butter. Whisk in the mustard and tarragon. Adjust the seasoning and add a squeeze of lemon juice.

TO FINISH: Add the stuffed lettuce rolls to the sauce and reheat. Heat a frying pan over medium and add 1 tbsp (15 ml) olive oil and 1 tbsp (15 ml) butter. Once the butter begins to brown, add the shallot and garlic. Stir until fragrant and add the mushrooms and sauté for 2 minutes. Season with salt and pepper and add parsley. In a large frying pan on medium-high, add the remaining 2 tbsp (30 ml) olive oil. Depending on the size of your pan, cook the filets in 2 or 3 batches. Cook skin-side down for 3 to 4 minutes. Flip over and remove pan from heat. Wait 30 seconds and remove filets from pan.

TO ASSEMBLE: Place some potato purée in the centre of each plate. Make a 5-inch (13 cm) streak through the purée with the back of a spoon. Place a trout filet skin-side up on top of the purée. Arrange a spoonful of chanterelle mushrooms on the filet and top with a second filet. Place a lettuce roll beside the fish and finish with the tarragon-mustard sauce.

Serves 4

Nutritional Value Per Serving (421 g): Calories 618, Protein 30 g, Carbohydrates 20 g, Dietary Fibre 2.2 g, Sugars 2.3 g, Total Fat 40 g, Saturated Fat 15.6 g, Cholesterol 129 mg, Sodium 440 mg

CHEF'S CHOICE:
Noily Pratt

Roasted Halibut with Oyster Tagliatelle, Fennel Confit and Caviar

4 6-oz (170 g) halibut portions
(when cleaning, reserve the trim)

7 oz (200 g) pasta dough, rolled and cut into tagliatelle, or use dried

4 celery stalks, peeled and cut into
⅛-inch x 1-inch (3 mm x 2½ cm) batons

2 plum tomatoes, blanched, peeled,
seeded and diced

2 tsp (10 ml) caviar (optional)

FENNEL CONFIT:

1 fennel bulb, diced small,
green shoots reserved

1½ tbsp (22 ml) olive oil

¼ cup (65 ml) Pernod

Salt and freshly ground pepper

SAUCE:

12 oysters

2 shallots, finely sliced

1 small garlic clove, finely sliced

4 button mushrooms, finely sliced

3½ oz (100 g) fish trim

⅓ cup (85 ml) good vermouth

⅔ cup (170 ml) fish stock

¾ cup (190 ml) whipping cream

Squeeze of lemon (optional)

FENNEL CONFIT: Heat ½ tbsp (7 ml) of the olive oil in a small saucepan on medium. Add the fennel and season with a pinch of salt and pepper. Stir gently for 3 to 4 minutes, until soft. Deglaze with Pernod and stir until liquid has evaporated. Check seasoning.

SAUCE: Shuck the oysters and strain, reserving the juice. Wash the oyster meat and reserve. Heat ½ tbsp (7 ml) of olive oil in a medium-size saucepan on medium. Add the shallots, garlic and fennel shoots and sauté for 2 to 3 minutes. Add the mushrooms and fish trim; cover and sweat for 4 to 5 minutes. Add the vermouth, reducing by half before adding the fish stock. Reduce by half again. Add the cream, cover and bring to a boil. Add the reserved oyster juice. Check seasoning and let stand, uncovered, for 20 minutes. Once the mixture has cooled, pass through a fine strainer and adjust seasoning. A little lemon juice can be added for acidity and freshness, if needed. Return to pan.

TO ASSEMBLE: Heat oven to 400°F (200°C). Place a medium-size pot half-filled with salted water on the stove to boil. Season the halibut with salt and pepper. In a large oven-safe non-stick frying pan, heat ½ tbsp (7 ml) of the olive oil over high. Place halibut in the pan and put in oven for 6 to 8 minutes. Place pasta in water and bring back to a boil. Cook until tender. Fresh pasta takes 3 to 5 minutes; dried takes a little longer so blanch beforehand. Bring the sauce to a simmer and add the celery. Let simmer for 1 minute before adding the oyster meat and tomatoes. Drain pasta well, then add to the sauce. Spoon portions of pasta/sauce into bowls. Remove halibut from the oven, turn fish over, season with salt and pepper and drain on paper towel. Place fish on top of pasta and spoon the fennel confit on top. Finish with caviar, if using.

Serves 4

Nutritional Value Per Serving (680 g): Calories 724, Protein 58 g, Carbohydrates 42 g, Dietary Fibre 4.2 g, Sugars 4.3 g, Total Fat 33 g, Saturated Fat 13 g, Cholesterol 257 mg, Sodium 600 mg

SUGGESTED WINE PAIRING:
Jackson-Triggs Proprietors' Grand Reserve Chardonnay
Named Winery of the Year by Wine Access magazine in 2008
Awarded Silver in the Pacific Rim International Wine Competition
Aromas of ripe tropical fruit, butterscotch and toasted oak with a creamy buttery finish

Cured Swordfish
with Meyer Lemon Vinaigrette

1 centre-cut swordfish loin,
about 1½ lbs (680 g)

CURING MIXTURE:

¼ cup (65 ml) cinnamon

¼ cup (65 ml) whole black peppercorns

2 tbsp (30 ml) coriander seeds

2 tbsp (30 ml) cloves

1 tbsp (15 ml) fennel seeds

1 tsp (5 ml) star anis

1½ lbs (680 g) kosher salt

8 garlic cloves, chopped

¼ cup (65 ml) thyme, chopped

VINAIGRETTE:

2 small Meyer lemons

1 blood orange, broken into segments

1 small shallot, finely chopped

2 tbsp (30 ml) finely chopped chives

⅓ cup (85 ml) extra-virgin olive oil

GARNISHES: 1 bunch chervil, soaked in ice
water for 10 minutes, pistachio oil

To cure the swordfish, start the day ahead. In a medium-size frying pan, toast the cinnamon, peppercorns, coriander seeds, cloves, fennel seeds and star anise over medium heat for 5 to 10 minutes, stirring occasionally until the fennel seeds turn dark. Transfer to a spice or coffee grinder and reduce to a powder using the pulse setting. In a small mixing bowl, combine the spice powder with the salt, garlic and thyme. You need only one-third of the total for this recipe, but the remainder can be stored in a well-sealed container for up to 1 year. Roll the swordfish in the curing mixture, then wrap tightly in plastic and leave in the refrigerator for 24 hours. The next day, rinse the swordfish under cool running water for 20 to 25 minutes. Let dry on a cheesecloth.

VINAIGRETTE: Remove the segments from the Meyer lemons, reserving the juice. In a small mixing bowl, combine the lemon juice and segments with the blood orange segments, shallots and chives. Add the olive oil and mix well.

TO ASSEMBLE: Slice the swordfish into ⅛-inch (3 mm) portions and arrange on plates. Pour vinaigrette evenly over each portion, ensuring that each plate has an equal amount of lemon and blood orange segments. Garnish with chervil. Drizzle with pistachio oil if using.

Serves 4

Nutritional Value Per Serving (454 g): Calories 464, Protein 36 g, Carbohydrates 22 g, Dietary Fibre 9.5 g, Sugars 3.8 g, Total Fat 27 g, Saturated Fat 4.7 g, Cholesterol 66 mg, Sodium 2150 mg

Miso-Crusted Sablefish

4 4-oz (115 g) portions sablefish, skin on

½ cup (125 ml) miso paste

2 tbsp (30 ml) sake

1½ cups (375 ml) sugar

1 cup (250 ml) shiitake mushrooms, thinly sliced

16 oz (450 g) soba noodles

3 green onions, thinly sliced

BROTH:

8 cups (2 L) water

2 tbsp (30 ml) roughly chopped ginger

1 tbsp (15 ml) sliced lemongrass

½ piece dried seaweed

½ cup (125 ml) bonito flakes, packed

1 tbsp (15 ml) light soy sauce

¾ tbsp (10 ml) rice vinegar

BROTH: In a medium-size saucepan, add water, ginger, lemongrass and dried seaweed and bring to a simmer. Add the bonito flakes and reduce to low. Simmer for 3 minutes and then turn off heat. Let stand, uncovered, for 30 minutes. Add the soy sauce and rice vinegar. Strain through a fine sieve and reserve.

MISO CRUST AND SABLEFISH: Heat oven to 400°F (200°C). Simmer the miso paste and sake in a medium-size saucepan, whisking until the sake is incorporated. Whisk in the sugar. Remove from heat and let stand for 30 minutes to dissolve the sugar. When the marinade has cooled, add the sablefish and let stand for 30 minutes. Remove the sablefish and place on a baking tray skin-side down. Cook for 8 minutes. The fish should be lightly caramelized. Remove from oven and take the skin off with a spatula.

TO ASSEMBLE: While the fish is in the oven, cook the noodles until al dente and refresh in cold water. When the fish is almost done, heat the broth and divide among the bowls. Place equal amounts of noodles and mushrooms in each bowl. Arrange the sablefish on top, crusted-side up, and garnish with the sliced green onions.

Serves 4

Substitution: Cod or halibut may also be used.

Nutritional Value Per Serving (1765 g): Calories 751, Protein 49 g, Carbohydrates 95 g, Dietary Fibre 1.7 g, Sugars 4.3 g, Total Fat 20 g, Saturated Fat 3.9 g, Cholesterol 72 mg, Sodium 3222 mg

SUGGESTED WINE PAIRING:
Sumac Ridge Estate Winery White Meritage
A blend of 80% Sauvignon Blanc and 20% Semillon,
this wine is typical of the style of the great white wines of Bordeaux.

Mussels

Seafood Ceviche

1 oz (30 g) white fish such as red snapper, flounder, sea bass or grouper, thinly sliced

1 oz (30 g) salmon, thinly sliced

5 shrimps, peeled, deveined and blanched

2 large scallops, thinly sliced

5 clams or mussels

2 tsp (10 ml) minced red onion

10 leaves each mint and cilantro, chopped

SAUCE:

2 Thai red chili peppers, finely chopped

1 garlic clove, finely chopped

2 tbsp (30 ml) lime juice

1 tbsp (15 ml) water

2 tsp (10 ml) Thai fish sauce

Pinch salt

Bring about 4 cups (1 L) water to a boil and add the clams or mussels. Cover and cook for 5 minutes or until they open. Discard any that don't open. Quickly cool in ice water, drain and set aside until ready to use. To make the sauce, combine all the ingredients. Immerse the fish and clams and marinate for 5 minutes. Immediately divide among the plates and top with the red onion and herbs.

Serves 1 or 2

Chef's note: The ingredient in the sauce that "cooks" the fish is the lime juice.

Nutritional Value Per Serving (403 g): Calories 225, Protein 34 g, Carbohydrates 16 g, Dietary Fibre 5.5 g, Sugars 5.1 g, Total Fat 3.4 g, Saturated Fat 0.5 g, Cholesterol 102 mg, Sodium 3256 mg

East Coast Scallops

12 U-10 fresh sea scallops

Kosher salt and freshly ground pepper

1 tbsp (15 ml) equal mix of butter and olive oil

Parsley and thyme, finely chopped, for various uses

¼ cup (65 ml) butter, for various uses

1 shallot, finely diced

4 oz (120 g) butternut squash, diced small

2 garlic cloves, minced

½ cup (125 ml) chicken stock

Small bunch rainbow chard, julienned

2 tbsp (30 ml) dry white wine

¼ cup (65 ml) 1% milk

DUPUY LENTILS:

13 oz (360 g) Dupuy lentils

8 cups (2 L) chicken stock

1 large onion, chopped

1 large carrot, chopped

½ celery stalk, chopped

4 garlic cloves

Spice bag: 2 bay leaves, 4 sprigs each rosemary and thyme, 25 black peppercorns

BUTTERNUT SQUASH PURÉE:

1 butternut squash, sliced in half lengthwise, seeds removed

1-2 tbsp (15-30 ml) olive oil

CREAMED "COOKSTOWN" SALSIFY:

1 large white onion, roughly chopped

1 tbsp (15 ml) olive oil

6 large salsify, trimmed, peeled, roughly chopped

1 garlic clove, minced

1 cup (250 ml) dry white wine

2 cups (500 ml) 35% cream

Spice bag: 1 bay leaf, 3 sprigs thyme, 10 black peppercorns

ARTICHOKE FOAM:

3 shallots, chopped

1 tbsp (15 ml) olive oil

10 oz (290 g) artichoke hearts, roughly chopped, or use 1 medium-size can

3 garlic cloves, minced

1 cup (250 ml) dry white wine

2 cups (500 ml) 35% cream

Spice bag: 1 bay leaf, 3 sprigs thyme, 10 black peppercorns

DUPUY LENTILS: Place the ingredients and spice bag in a large pot and cook at a simmer until al dente. Discard spice bag and strain. Dry on a baking sheet in the fridge.

BUTTERNUT SQUASH PURÉE: Heat oven to 350°F (180°C). Brush the inside of the 2 halves with the oil and season with salt and pepper. Place on a baking sheet cut-side down and bake for 45 minutes or until tender. Purée the flesh in a blender.

CREAMED "COOKSTOWN" SALSIFY: Sweat onions in oil on medium until translucent. Add salsify and garlic and cook 1 minute, without browning. Add wine and spice bag. Reduce by half, turn heat to medium-low and add the cream. Cook, uncovered, for 45 minutes or until salsify is tender. Discard spice bag and purée until smooth. Season with salt.

ARTICHOKE FOAM: Sweat the shallots in the olive oil over medium heat for 1 minute, without browning. Stir in the artichokes and garlic and cook for 1 minute. Deglaze with the white wine and add the spice bag. Still at medium, reduce by half. Add the cream and simmer, uncovered, for 7 minutes. Discard the spice bag and blend until smooth. Pass through a fine sieve and season with salt. Will be transformed into a foam just before serving.

SCALLOPS: Heat oven to 375°F (190°C). Pat scallops dry and season with salt and pepper. Heat the butter-oil mixture on medium-high until bubbles form. Sear the scallops until golden-brown. Turn over and place pan in the oven. Cook for 3½ to 4 minutes, until slightly firm. Sprinkle with parsley and thyme.

TO ASSEMBLE: Melt 1 tbsp (15 ml) butter over medium-high heat. Sauté half the shallots and all the diced butternut squash for 1 minute. Add half the garlic, chicken stock, cooked Dupuy lentils and butternut squash purée and simmer until stock is absorbed. Season with salt, pepper, parsley and thyme.

To wilt the chard, bring 1 tbsp (15 ml) butter to a bubble in a pan over medium-high heat. Add remaining shallots and sweat for 1 minute. Add chard and cook 30 seconds. Deglaze with the wine and add remaining garlic. Season with salt and pepper. Drain on a towel before plating. In a saucepan on low, heat the cooled salsify purée and half the milk until hot. Season with salt. Warm the turnips in a lightly buttered pan over medium heat, without browning. Season with salt, parsley and thyme. Cut each turnip in half.

Bring the artichoke purée and the remaining milk to a light simmer over medium-low heat. Season with salt. Once everything has been arranged on the plate, add a knob of butter to the pot and foam the liquid with a hand-held blender. Ladle the foam over the scallops.

Serves 4

Nutritional Value Per Serving (923 g): Calories 1645, Protein 84 g, Carbohydrates 145 g, Dietary Fibre 13 g, Sugars 6.8 g, Total Fat 78 g, Saturated Fat 32 g, Cholesterol 692 mg, Sodium 1304 mg

SUGGESTED WINE PAIRING:
Remy Pannier (AOC)
Muscadet De Sevre Maine
www.eurovintage.com

Rutabaga

Seared Tuna with Ragoût de Légumes aux Épices Marocains

AUBERGE *du* POMMIER

SEARED TUNA:
1 8-oz (225 g) piece tuna
Salt and freshly ground pepper
Fine cornmeal, for coating
½ cup (125 ml) vegetable oil

RAGOÛT DE LÉGUMES:
1 tbsp (15 ml) vegetable or canola oil
½ cup (125 ml) diced carrots
½ cup (125 ml) diced rutabaga
½ cup (125 ml) diced celeriac
½ cup (125 ml) parsnip, diced small

½ cup (125 ml) onion, diced small
½ cup (125 ml) leek, diced small
3 garlic cloves, sliced
2 bay leaves, cracked
3 pieces star anise
½ cinnamon stick
1 pinch each nutmeg and turmeric
1 cup (250 ml) chopped tomato, skin and seeds removed, or canned tomato
¼ cup (65 ml) chopped cilantro
Salt and freshly ground pepper
Chili or herb oil, to garnish

SPICY PINEAPPLE YOGURT:
(mix all the ingredients together)
½ cup (125 ml) organic plain yogurt
1 tbsp (15 ml) diced fresh pineapple
Pinch ground coriander
Splash lime juice
Splash green Tabasco (optional)

RAGOÛT DE LÉGUMES: Add the oil to a large frying pan set on medium-low heat. Sweat the vegetables and spices in the oil until tender and fragrant, making sure not to brown. Add the tomato and turn up heat. Cook, uncovered, at a simmer until the mixture resembles a ragout. If it becomes too dry, add a bit of water or vegetable or chicken stock. Adjust the seasoning as necessary. Before serving, mix in the cilantro.

TUNA: Season with salt and pepper. Coat the tuna on all sides with the cornmeal. Pour oil into a medium-size pan and place over medium heat until hot. Sear the tuna for 30 seconds on each side. Remove from pan and cover with foil until ready to serve, at which time cut into ¼-inch (6 mm) slices.

TO ASSEMBLE: Spoon a portion of ragout onto each plate. Drizzle with oil if using. Layer tuna slices on top and add a dollop of pineapple yogurt.

Serves 1

Chef's note: The ragout can be served with roast lamb, but mix in some raisins, apricots or dates when you add the tomato.
We like to garnish this dish with onion rings.

Nutritional Value Per Serving (1246 g): Calories 1713, Protein 69 g, Carbohydrates 80 g, Dietary Fibre 16 g, Sugars 34 g,
Total Fat 22 g, Saturated Fat 3.5 g, Cholesterol 9.6 mg, Sodium 1600 mg

SUGGESTED WINE PAIRING:
Louis Latour Bourgogne Pinot Noir
Burgundy, France
Represented by Mark Anthony Brands
www.markanthony.com

Maple Syrup-Glazed
Cedar Roast Salmon with Fingerling Potatoes and Red Onion Marmalade

THE *Fairmont*
CHATEAU WHISTLER

4 6-oz (170 g) portions salmon, preferably wild sockeye

4 cedar papers, soaked in warm water *(see note)*

2 tbsp (30 ml) olive oil

1 cup (250 ml) kosher salt

½ cup (125 ml) maple syrup

Zest of 1 lemon and 1 orange

½ tsp (2 ml) freshly cracked pepper

FINGERLINGS:

1 lb (450 g) fingerling potatoes, cut in half lengthwise

2 tbsp (30 ml) olive oil

2 tbsp (30 ml) Pommery mustard

Sea salt and freshly cracked pepper

RED ONION MARMALADE:

1 medium red onion, julienned

½ cup (125 ml) red wine vinegar

½ cup (125 ml) honey

2 sprigs thyme

CURING THE SALMON: Combine the kosher salt, maple syrup, zests and pepper in a bowl, then spread a thin layer on a baking sheet. Place the salmon top-side down on the cure. Cover and put in the refrigerator for 1 hour. Heat oven to 350°F (180°C). Remove the salmon and wipe off excess cure. In a large frying pan, heat the olive oil on medium-high and lightly sear the bottom side of the salmon. Wrap each portion in a cedar paper, tie with twine and place on a baking sheet. Bake for 5 to 7 minutes.

FINGERLINGS: Heat oven to 400°F (200°C). Toss the potatoes with olive oil and salt and pepper to taste and roast until tender. Toss with the mustard. This dish can be prepared in advance and reheated a few minutes before serving. If preparing potatoes in advance be sure to toss with mustard only after reheating.

RED ONION MARMALADE: Place the onion in a small saucepan and add the vinegar, honey and thyme. Bring to a simmer and reduce until the liquid reaches a syrupy consistency.

Serves 4

Chef's note: The maple syrup we use is aged for 2 months in our own Canadian oak whisky barrels, but any good-quality maple syrup will work well in this recipe. If you can't find cedar papers at your supermarket, most specialty food stores will have them.

Suggested side dish: Lightly steam about 1 lb (450 g) of seasonal vegetables such as green beans or sugar snap peas and toss with 2 tbsp (30 ml) extra-virgin olive oil, a handful of fine herbs such as flat leaf parsley, chervil or thyme, and salt and pepper to taste.

Nutritional Value Per Serving (505 g): Calories 796, Protein 40 g, Carbohydrates 88 g, Dietary Fibre 2.5 g, Sugars 59 g, Total Fat 28 g, Saturated Fat 4.4 g, Cholesterol 105 mg, Sodium 1451 mg

SUGGESTED WINE PAIRING:
Dan Aykroyd Discovery Series Pinot Noir
Light and refreshing with subtle cedar notes
www.DanAykroydWines.com

Seafood Platter

Scallops, served raw

Oysters, served raw

Clam meat, already cooked

Shrimp

1½ cups (375 ml) kosher salt

½ bottle Tabasco sauce

Juice of 2 lemons

COCKTAIL SAUCE:
(mix all the ingredients together)

2 cups (500 ml) ketchup

1 cup (250 ml) grated celery

1 cup (250 ml) freshly grated horseradish

1 tbsp (15 ml) store-bought white horseradish

Salt and freshly ground pepper

1 oz (30 g) cognac

¼ cup (65 ml) Worcestershire sauce

2 tbsp (30 ml) Tabasco sauce

Juice of 3 lemons

MIGNONETTE:
(mix all the ingredients together)

2 shallots, finely chopped

½ cup (125 ml) red wine vinegar

1 tbsp (15 ml) freshly cracked pepper

To prepare the shrimp, add salt to 12 cups (3 L) of water along with the Tabasco and lemon juice. Bring to a boil. Add shrimp and cook for 45 seconds to 1 minute. Turn off heat and add to a bucket of ice to cool everything down quickly. Remove the shrimp and then remove their shells. Arrange all of the seafood on a platter and serve with the cocktail sauce and mignonette.

Nutritional Value Per Serving (437 g): Calories 218, Protein 12 g, Carbohydrates 45 g, Dietary Fibre 2.3 g, Sugars 32 g, Total Fat 1.5 g, Saturated Fat 0.23 g, Cholesterol 39 mg, Sodium 9023 mg

Oven-Roasted Halibut
with Soba Noodle Salad and
Roasted Pineapple Sauce

LOBBY ON YORK

6 6-oz (170 g) halibut filets, skin removed

Salt and freshly ground pepper

7 tbsp (105 ml) water or veal stock

1 tsp (5 ml) garlic butter

SAKE SAUCE:

1 cup (250 ml) chicken stock

2 tbsp (30 ml) soy sauce

2 tbsp (30 ml) sweetened rice vinegar

2 tbsp (30 ml) dry sake

1 tsp (5 ml) sesame oil

3 oz (85 g) shiitake mushrooms, sliced

1 tbsp (15 ml) minced lemongrass

1 green onion, whites only, thinly sliced

¼ cup (65 ml) sugar

Pinch dry chili flakes

ROASTED PINEAPPLE SAUCE:

1 tbsp (15 ml) canola oil

¼ pineapple, cubed large

½ red onion, diced large

3 garlic cloves

2 tbsp (30 ml) brown sugar

1 cup (250 ml) canned plum tomatoes, drained

1 tsp (5 ml) fish sauce

Juice of 1 lime

SOBA NOODLE SALAD:

1 carrot, zucchini and cucumber, each cut into ribbons with a potato peeler

Sprigs dill

Celery and mint leaves

Head frisée lettuce, yellow inner part only, separated into sprigs

2 bunches soba noodles

Optional garnishes: shredded green onion, jicama, daikon or radicchio, lemon oil

SAKE SAUCE: Bring the ingredients to a boil, whisking constantly. Turn off heat immediately and set aside. ROASTED PINEAPPLE SAUCE: Heat a saucepan on high and sauté the pineapple, onion and garlic until the pineapple begins to caramelize. Add the brown sugar, tomatoes, fish sauce, lime juice and cook for 3 minutes. Transfer to a blender and purée. Season with salt and pepper. SOBA NOODLE SALAD: In a pot of salted water, blanch the carrot and zucchini separately until just tender. Cool in an ice bath and then drain. Toss with the cucumber and other salad ingredients. To cook the noodles, bring 8 cups (2 L) water to a boil. Add the noodles and cook until just tender, 1 to 2 minutes. Drain and toss with salad mixture. HALIBUT: Heat oven to 500°F (260°C). Place fish in a lightly oiled baking dish just large enough to hold all 6 pieces. Season with salt and pepper and cover with sake sauce and water or veal stock. Place garlic butter on top and bake, uncovered, for 10 minutes. Divide among the plates.

TO ASSEMBLE: Top the halibut with the mushrooms from the baking dish. Add the liquid from the baking dish to the noodle salad and toss to distribute. Using tongs, twist the noodle salad into 6 bundles and place beside the fish. Add a dollop of the roasted pineapple sauce to each plate and garnish the fish according to your taste.

Serves 6

Substitution: Black cod or sea bass may be used instead of halibut.

Nutritional Value Per Serving (487 g): Calories 333, Protein 39 g, Carbohydrates 25 g, Dietary Fibre 3.1 g, Sugars 19 g, Total Fat 8.1 g, Saturated Fat 1.2 g, Cholesterol 56 mg, Sodium 892 mg

Desserts

Lemon

Natas do Ceu
Cream of Heaven

Chiado
Fine Dining

2 cups (500 ml) sugar

1½ tbsp (22 ml) cornstarch

¼ cup (65 ml) water

12 eggs, separated

Rind 1 lemon

2 cups (500 ml) 35% cream

3½ oz (100 g) crushed ladyfingers, almond biscotti or other plain cookie

3 oz (85 g) almond liqueur (optional)

Garnishes: raspberries, raspberry coulis, meringues, crispy almond biscotti, fresh mint

EGG SWEET: Use a stainless steel pot that is completely free of fat. Set the pot over low heat. Add 1¾ cups (440 ml) of the sugar to the pot and heat, stirring constantly, to a pearl consistency. This may take a while so be patient. Remove from heat. In a small bowl, whisk the cornstarch and water. Whisk in the egg yolks and mix well. Put through a sieve 3 times to make sure it is ultra smooth. Scrape the entire egg yolk mixture onto the warm sugar in the pot and fold in. Stir in the lemon rind. Turn the heat back to low and slowly bring to a simmer, stirring constantly. As soon as the first bubbles appear, remove from heat and place in a bowl to cool. Cover until ready to use.

EGG WHITE-CREAM MIXTURE: Beat the cream until stiff. Set aside. Beat the egg whites until soft peaks form. Add the remaining ¼ cup (65 ml) of sugar and beat a little longer until the sugar is blended in and the peaks are stiff. Fold the egg whites and whipped cream together.

TO ASSEMBLE: Start by placing half of the crushed cookies in the bottom of a serving dish. Sprinkle evenly with the liqueur. Arrange half of the egg white-cream mixture over the base, then sprinkle the remaining crushed cookies over the mixture. Add the remaining egg white-cream mixture. Freeze for at least 1 hour. Right before serving, pour the egg sweet over the top.

Serves 6

Nutritional Value Per Serving (219 g): Calories 538, Protein 13 g, Carbohydrates 64 g, Dietary Fibre 0.7 g, Sugars 53.7 g, Total Fat 26 g, Saturated Fat 12.6 g, Cholesterol 427 mg, Sodium 236 mg

Chocolate Salame with Zabaglione Sauce

7 oz (200 g) butter

7 oz (200 g) sugar

3½ oz (100 g) cocoa

5½ oz (160 g) hazelnuts, crushed

2 tbsp (30 ml) grappa

2 tbsp (30 ml) amaretto liqueur

10½ oz (300 g) arrowroot cookies, coarsely crumbled

3½ oz (100 g) Italian amaretti cookies, coarsely crumbled

2 eggs

1 egg yolk

Garnishes: white chocolate stick, chocolate shavings, mint leaves

ZABAGLIONE SAUCE:

4 egg yolks

¼ cup (65 ml) sugar

½ cup (125 ml) Marsala wine

Soften the butter to just above room temperature. In a bowl, mix together the sugar, hazelnuts, cocoa and 2 liqueurs. Add the arrowroot and amaretti cookies, then the butter. In a separate bowl, lightly whip the eggs. Add to the other ingredients. Work the mixture well to incorporate all of the ingredients. Pour onto a silicone mat or parchment paper. Roll into a salami shape and refrigerate for at least 2 hours. Cut into slices and serve with Zabaglione sauce.

ZABAGLIONE SAUCE: In a metal bowl, beat the egg yolks with the sugar until they become pale. Add the Marsala and mix well. In the bottom of a double boiler, bring water to just below the boiling point (boiling water will make the eggs taste burned). Add the egg mixture to the pan on top and whip for 2 to 3 minutes, until stiff peaks form.

Serves 15

Chef's note: If well wrapped, can be frozen for up to 3 months.

Nutritional Value Per Serving (96 g): Calories 403, Protein 6.7 g, Carbohydrates 44 g, Dietary Fibre 3.2 g, Sugars 21.8 g, Total Fat 23.5 g, Saturated Fat 8.7 g, Cholesterol 123 mg, Sodium 178 mg

chocolate

Pain Perdu with Strawberry-Rhubarb Purée

4 slices French toast

8 oz (225 g) strawberry-rhubarb purée

4 scoops vanilla ice cream

8 oz (225 g) fresh strawberries,
tops removed and sliced

2-3 tbsp (30-45 ml) sliced almonds,
lightly toasted

4 tbsp (60 ml) Canadian birch or maple syrup

Maple or cinnamon sugar, for dusting (make
cinnamon sugar by combining 2 parts icing
sugar with 1 part cinnamon)

Garnishes: mint leaves, edible flowers

STRAWBERRY-RHUBARB PURÉE:

¼ cup (65 ml) sugar

1 cup (250 ml) ¼-inch-thick (6 mm)
slices rhubarb

½ cup (125 ml) strawberries,
tops removed, quartered

Juice of ½ lime

FRENCH TOAST:

4½-inch-thick (12 mm) slices brioche
or baguette

6 eggs

2 cups (500 ml) 3% milk

2 tbsp (30 ml) sugar

1 vanilla bean, split lengthwise,
or 1 tsp (5 ml) vanilla

1 tbsp (15 ml) unsalted butter, softened

STRAWBERRY-RHUBARB PURÉE: Bring the sugar and rhubarb to a simmer in a non-reactive pot. Cook for 5 minutes, stirring occasionally. Add the strawberries and continue simmering for about 4 minutes, or until the strawberries break down. Remove from heat and let cool. Transfer to a blender and purée into a thick jam. Squeeze in the lime juice and stir. Can be made up to 1 day in advance.

FRENCH TOAST: Whisk the eggs in a medium bowl. Whisk in the milk and sugar. Add the vanilla bean. Soak the bread slices in the mixture for a few minutes. Melt the butter in a frying pan on medium heat and sauté the bread slices on each side until golden-brown.

TO ASSEMBLE: This dish is improved when the plates are warmed in advance. Place a slice of French toast on each plate. Spoon the purée on and around the toast. Top with the ice cream, sliced strawberries and almonds. Drizzle with syrup. Dust with maple or cinnamon sugar and garnish.

Serves 4

Chef's note: Be sure to use fruit that is in season. Peaches work great as well. For vanilla-flavoured sugar, remove the vanilla bean from the French toast mixture and rinse and dry well, then place in a bowl of sugar. For a different garnish, try chantilly cream and a dusting of icing sugar.

Nutritional Value Per Serving (440 g): Calories 567, Protein 19.8 g, Carbohydrates 75 g, Dietary Fibre 3.7 g, Sugars 50 g,
Total Fat 23 g, Saturated Fat 10.9 g, Cholesterol 328 mg, Sodium 406 mg

SUGGESTED WINE PAIRING:
2008 Stratus Icewine Red
Individual hand-harvesting of 3 red varieties, Cabernet Sauvignon,
Cabernet Franc and Syrah are combined into this signature assemblage Icewine.
A rich and refreshing long finish.

Goat Cheese Cake
with Caramel Sauce
and Crushed Amaretti

The Only
On King

1 tbsp (15 ml) unsalted butter, softened

3 cups (750 ml) goat cheese, 15% milk fat, 68% moisture

1½ cups (375 ml) mascarpone cheese

¾ cup (190 ml) sugar, plus 3 tbsp (45 ml)

3 eggs

6 egg yolks

½ tsp (2 ml) vanilla

Amaretti biscuits, coarsely crushed, to garnish

CARAMEL SAUCE:

1 cup (250 ml) sugar

1 cup (250 ml) 35% cream

Heat oven to 325°F (160°C). Rub the bottom and sides of a 12-inch (30 cm) springform pan with the butter and dust with 3 tbsp (45 ml) of the sugar. Wrap a piece of foil around the bottom and up the sides of the pan. In a mixer with a paddle, combine the goat cheese, mascarpone and remaining sugar until smooth and creamy. In a separate bowl, beat the eggs and vanilla until combined. Add to the cheese mixture and mix well. Pass through a sieve into the springform pan. Cover with foil and set in a deep baking pan. Pour hot water into the pan until it reaches halfway up the sides of the springform pan. Bake for 20 minutes, rotate and bake for 20 minutes more. Remove from the water bath and put in the fridge overnight to set. Just before serving, remove from pan and slice. Garnish with caramel sauce and amaretti pieces.

CARAMEL SAUCE: While the cake is baking, place the sugar in a large saucepan over medium heat and cook, uncovered, until it becomes liquid and then caramel in colour. Stir only once it caramelizes. This should take about 5 minutes. Be very careful because liquid sugar can cause severe burns. Remove from heat and slowly add the cream, whisking throughout. Continue whisking until well combined. Remove to a container, cover and chill in the fridge overnight. Can be stored in the fridge for 5 days.

Nutritional Value Per Serving (148 g): Calories 541, Protein 13.3 g, Carbohydrates 25 g, Dietary Fibre 0 g, Sugars 46 g, Total Fat 26 g, Saturated Fat 26 g, Cholesterol 274 mg, Sodium 203 mg

SUGGESTED WINE PAIRING:
2007 Harvest Gold, Rosewood Estates winery and meadery
Fragrant tones of white flowers, almond and toffee with a luscious, velvety palate
From Niagara's only meadery producing world class meads and award-winning wines of Riesling, Semillon and Pinot Noir
www.rosewoodwine.com

Almond

Pear and Cranberry Almond Crumble

ALMOND CRUMBLE:

2 tbsp (30 ml) ground almonds

2 tbsp (30 ml) cake flour

2 tbsp (30 ml) sugar

2 tbsp (30 ml) cold butter, diced

FRUIT BASE:

1 tbsp (15 ml) butter

2 tsp (10 ml) brown sugar

1 tsp (5 ml) lemon juice

¼ tsp (1 ml) orange zest

¼ tsp (1 ml) lemon zest

Pinch vanilla powder

¼ cup (65 ml) fresh or dried cranberries *(see note)*

3 Anjou pears, peeled and diced

Heat oven to 350°F (180°C). In a medium-size bowl, combine all of the almond crumble ingredients until a crumble consistency is formed. Refrigerate. For the fruit base, melt the butter on medium heat and add the sugar, lemon juice, both zests and vanilla. Stir in the cranberries and pears and caramelize, cooking for approximately 5 to 10 minutes. Transfer to ramekins and cover with the almond crumble. Bake for 20 minutes, until the crumble is light brown. Best served with ice cream.

Serves 2 to 3

Chef's note: If using dried cranberries, bring cranberry or orange juice to a boil and pour over the cranberries. Let soak for 30 minutes. Do the same if using frozen cranberries.

Nutritional Value Per Serving (409 g): Calories 465, Protein 3.3 g, Carbohydrates 75 g, Dietary Fibre 12 g, Sugars 48.5 g, Total Fat 21 g, Saturated Fat 11.2 g, Cholesterol 46 mg, Sodium 126 mg

lemon zest
brown sugar

Frozen Lemon Tamarind Soufflé with Toasted Meringue

west

FROZEN SOUFFLÉ:

¾ cup (190 ml) sugar

¼ cup (65 ml) lemon juice

2 tbsp (30 ml) lemon zest

3 eggs, separated

1 tbsp (15 ml) tamarind purée *(see note)*

2 tbsp (30 ml) honey

½ cup (125 ml) whipping cream

Pinch salt

MERINGUE:

⅓ cup (85 ml) egg whites

6 tbsp (90 ml) sugar

Zest of ½ lemon

FROZEN SOUFFLÉ: In a large stainless steel bowl, whisk together half the sugar, the lemon juice and zest, egg yolks, tamarind purée and honey. Place over a simmering water bath and keep whisking until mixture thickens, about 1 minute. Remove from water bath and cool to room temperature. In a separate bowl, whip the cream until soft peaks form. Fold the whipped cream into the lemon mixture. In a third bowl, whip the egg whites, salt and remaining sugar until medium-stiff peaks form. Fold into lemon-whipped cream mixture. Pipe into 6 6-oz ramekins and freeze overnight.

MERINGUE: Turn the oven to broil. Combine all of the ingredients in a stainless steel bowl and whisk over a simmering water bath until very warm to the touch. Remove from heat. Using an electric mixer, whisk until stiff peaks form.

TO ASSEMBLE: Place meringue in a piping bag with a large star tip. Remove ramekins from freezer and pipe meringue on top of the frozen soufflés. Place in oven for approximately 60 seconds, until meringue is browned, making sure that the soufflé doesn't melt. Serve immediately.

Serves 6

Chef's note: Tamarind purée is available at Indian grocery stores.

Nutritional Value Per Serving Size (103 g): Calories 224, Protein 4.7 g, Carbohydrates 35 g, Dietary Fibre 0.37 g, Sugars 33 g, Total Fat 9.6 g, Saturated Fat 5.3 g, Cholesterol 121 mg, Sodium 110 mg

cream honey

tamarind

Ten-Layer Coffee and Chocolate Cake

CinCin

CHOCOLATE GENOISE:

1 tbsp (15 ml) butter, melted

5 eggs

⅔ cup (170 ml) sugar

½ cup (125 ml) flour, plus some for dusting

2 tbsp (30 ml) cornstarch

1 tbsp (15 ml) unsweetened cocoa powder

COFFEE AND CHOCOLATE MOUSSE:

½ cup (125 ml) sugar

⅜ cup (95 ml) espresso
or other brewed coffee

4 egg yolks

1¼ cups (300 ml) 35% cream

9 oz (250 g) 70% chocolate

COFFEE SYRUP:

2 cups (500 ml) freshly brewed coffee

½ cup (125 ml) sugar

⅜ cup (95 ml) coffee-flavoured alcohol
such as Tia Maria

CHOCOLATE GLAZE:

1 cup (250 ml) 35% cream

6 oz (170 g) 70% chocolate, chopped

3 tbsp (45 ml) glucose or corn syrup

CHOCOLATE GENOISE: Heat oven to 350°F (180°C). With a pastry brush, butter the inside of a 10-inch (25 cm) cake pan, then dust with flour. Keep refrigerated. In a medium-size bowl, combine eggs and sugar over a simmering water bath. Whisk until frothy and hot. Remove from bath and continue whisking using an electric mixer. Begin at full speed and slowly reduce to medium, until mixture cools to room temperature and doubles in volume, 10 to 15 minutes. Sift the dry ingredients together and slowly incorporate into the egg-sugar mixture using a folding action. Pour into pan and bake for 25 minutes. Cool on counter to room temperature.

COFFEE AND CHOCOLATE MOUSSE: In a bowl set over a saucepan filled to the three-quarter mark with boiling water, continuously whisk sugar and espresso together to boiling point. Pour over egg yolks in a bowl and whisk until temperature lowers to 185°F (85°C). Pass through a fine sieve and cool by whisking with an electric mixer. This is called a sabayon. Set aside. Using an electric mixer with clean beaters, whip the cream until stiff peaks form. Set aside. In another bowl, melt the chocolate over simmering water, stirring constantly. Whisk in the sabayon and whipped cream. Remove from heat and let cool. Refrigerate for 30 minutes. Place in a piping bag.

COFFEE SYRUP: Combine the coffee with the sugar and add the alcohol to taste.

CHOCOLATE GLAZE: In a saucepan, bring cream to a boil. Remove from heat and incorporate chocolate. When creamy, stir in the glucose. Use glaze while still warm.

TO ASSEMBLE: With a serrated knife, slice the cake horizontally into 5 large discs plus a thin layer from the top of the genoise. Using a pastry brush, brush the layers with coffee syrup. Place 1 of the layers on a cake board and pipe the mousse on top to the same thickness as the layer. Add another layer and more mousse, repeating until you have 5 layers. Finish with the thin top layer. Place cake in fridge for 30 minutes. When well chilled, pour glaze overtop, making sure to cover sides. Put in fridge for 30 minutes or more. Transfer to a serving platter and touch up glaze if necessary.

Serves 12

Chef's note: This is not a difficult cake to make, just be patient because it is truly delicious. If you are left with extra mousse, it will stay in the fridge for 5 days, and the glaze for 2 weeks. You need not use all the coffee syrup. The more you use, the moister the cake will be, but too much will make it fall apart. For best results use stainless steel bowls.

Nutritional Value Per Serving (350 g), Calories 937, Protein 11.7 g, Carbohydrates 98 g, Dietary Fibre 3.9 g, Sugars 75 g, Total Fat 59 g, Saturated Fat 35 g, Cholesterol 343 mg, Sodium 168 mg

CHEF'S CHOICE:
Tia Maria

Raspberry Sablé with Raspberry Coulis and Chantilly Cream

4 cups (1 L) fresh raspberries

SABLÉ DOUGH (see note):

3¾ cups (940 ml) flour, sifted

7 oz (200 g) icing sugar,
plus some for sprinkling

1 vanilla bean, seeds only, pod discarded

Small pinch salt

14 oz (400 g) unsalted butter,
cut into 1-inch (2.5 cm) cubes, softened

1 tsp (5 ml) whipping cream

1 egg yolk

RASPBERRY COULIS:

2¼ cups (565 ml) fresh raspberries

¼ cup (65 g) sugar

Juice of 1 lemon

CHANTILLY CREAM:

1 cup (250 ml) whipping cream

1 tsp (5 ml) sugar

1 vanilla bean, seeds only, pod discarded

SABLÉ DOUGH: In a large bowl, whisk together the flour, icing sugar, vanilla and salt until well combined. Add the butter. Using your fingers or a pastry cutter, combine until the mixture resembles coarse oatmeal. Make a well in the centre and add the cream and egg. Combine gently just until the dough comes together. Turn onto a clean surface and flatten into a round. Cover well with plastic wrap and chill for 1 hour.

Heat oven to 350°F (180°C). On a lightly floured surface, roll out the dough until ¼ inch (6 mm) thick. Using a cutter 3 inches (7½ cm) in diameter, cut out about 40 discs. Place on a baking tray covered with parchment paper and refrigerate for 30 minutes. Bake for 12 to 20 minutes, depending on the thickness of the discs, or until golden-brown. Place on a cooling rack.

RASPBERRY COULIS: Combine the ingredients in a medium-size saucepan on medium heat. Stir constantly while bringing to a gentle boil. Simmer for 5 minutes, uncovered, still stirring occasionally, until mixture starts to thicken slightly. While still warm, purée and pass through a fine-mesh strainer. Chill before using.

CHANTILLY CREAM: Combine the cream, sugar and vanilla seeds in a mixer fitted with a whisk attachment. Whip until stiff peaks form.

TO ASSEMBLE: Toss the raspberries in a small amount of the raspberry coulis. Using the leftover raspberry coulis, decorate each plate. Arrange a ring of berries, approximately the diameter of the sablé discs, in the middle of the decoration. Spoon a small amount of the cream over the raspberries. Top with a sablé disc and repeat a second layer. Sprinkle with a bit of icing sugar and add one more dollop of cream.

Serves 6

Chef's note: The dough will yield about 40 cookies, but this recipe only uses 12.

Nutritional Value Per Serving (242 g): Calories 507, Protein 4.7 g, Carbohydrates 55.5 g, Dietary Fibre 9 g, Sugars 17 g, Total Fat 33 g, Saturated Fat 21 g, Cholesterol 115 mg, Sodium 35 mg

Tiramisu

1 cup (250 ml) sugar

2 cups (500 ml) 35% cream

6 egg yolks

18 oz (500 g) mascarpone cheese

½ cup (125 ml) finely chopped dark chocolate

1 cup (250 ml) espresso, at room temperature

¼ cup (65 ml) amaretto liqueur

1 bag ladyfinger cookies

Cocoa powder or chocolate shavings, for decoration

12 amaretti biscuits

Using a standing mixer at high speed, combine ½ cup (125 ml) of the sugar and the cream until soft peaks form. Set aside in the refrigerator. Beat the egg yolks at high speed with the remaining sugar until the ribbon stage. Reduce the speed and add the mascarpone, followed by the dark chocolate. As soon as the mascarpone and chocolate are mixed in, fold in the whipped cream until well incorporated.

Using a pastry bag, fill 12 martini glasses halfway with the mascarpone-cream mixture. In a shallow bowl, combine the espresso and amaretto. Working 1 at a time, dip both sides of each ladyfinger cookie into the liquid so the entire cookie is moist, making sure not to soak it. As you work, break the cookies into 3 or 4 pieces and place 2 or 3 pieces in each glass. Using the remaining mascarpone-cream mixture, fill each glass to the rim. Decorate with cocoa powder or chocolate shavings and arrange 1 amaretti biscuit on top. Place in fridge to set for at least 12 hours.

Serves 12

Chef's note: This dessert is gorgeous served in martini glasses, but a traditional presentation, as seen in the photo, is beautiful too. Any way you serve it, tiramisu is a great way to end a meal.

Nutritional Value Per Serving (169 g): Calories 567, Protein 9 g, Carbohydrates 43 g, Dietary Fibre 2.3 g, Sugars 23 g, Total Fat 42 g, Saturated Fat 23 g, Cholesterol 249 mg, Sodium 94 mg

White Chocolate and Vanilla Cream with Oranges

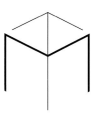

2½ cups (625 ml) 35% cream

1 vanilla pod

9 oz (250 g) white chocolate, chopped

4 egg yolks

3 gelatin sheets

4 large oranges

Put cream and vanilla pod in a saucepan and bring to a boil on high heat. Pour over white chocolate, egg yolks and gelatin in a bowl. Using a hand blender, start mixing immediately so the eggs don't begin cooking. Mix until smooth and divide among the dessert dishes. Refrigerate for about 1½ hours, or until the cream mixture is set. Peel the oranges with a knife and carve out the flesh. Arrange on top of the dessert.

Serves 10

Nutritional Value Per Serving (166 g): Calories 406, Protein 5.3 g, Carbohydrates 24.7 g, Dietary Fibre 1.8 g, Sugars 21 g, Total Fat 33 g, Saturated Fat 19.8 g, Cholesterol 171 mg, Sodium 54 mg

vanilla

Mango

Bakeapple
Cream Puffs

Bacalao

1 cup (250 ml) water

½ cup (125 ml) butter

1 cup (250 ml) flour

4 eggs

1 tbsp (15 ml) cloudberry liqueur *(see note)*

Sprig mint, to garnish

FRUIT TOPPING:

1 cup (250 ml) bakeapples

1 mango, diced

1 cup (250 ml) chopped fresh pineapple

½ cup (125 ml) sugar

WHIPPED CREAM FILLING:

1 cup (250 ml) 35% whipping cream

2-3 tbsp (30-45 ml) sugar

Heat oven to 375°F (190°C). In a medium saucepan set on medium-high heat, boil the water and butter. When the butter has melted, add the flour all at once. Stir with a wooden spoon until the mixture comes together in a ball. Transfer to a mixing bowl. Beat in the eggs, with a beater or by hand, 1 at a time until incorporated. The dough will be a little sticky. Divide into 8 mounds, dropping them onto well-greased baking sheets, making sure to leave 2 to 3 inches (5 to 10 cm) between mounds. They should be about 3 inches (7½ cm) around and 1½ inches (4 cm) high. Bake for about 25 minutes, until golden, firm and hollow-looking. Poke a hole near the bottom of each puff and return to oven for another 5 minutes to dry out. Cool on a rack. Can be made a day or 2 ahead and stored in an airtight container.

To make the topping, simmer the fruit and sugar over medium heat until the fruit has softened and the mixture has thickened, 10 to 15 minutes. Taste and adjust the flavour as desired, adding lemon juice if too sweet, more sugar if too tart. Cool. Can be made ahead and stored in a jar in the fridge. While the topping is cooling, make the filling by whipping together the cream, sugar and cloudberry liqueur until firm peaks form.

TO ASSEMBLE: Just before serving, cut the cream puffs in half laterally. Fill the bottom half with whipped cream and replace the top. Spoon the topping over and add a few more dollops of whipped cream. Garnish with a slice of pineapple, mango or a sprig of fresh mint.

Serves 8

Chef's note: The berries Newfoundlanders call bakeapples are known as cloudberries in Scandinavia. They look like small, amber-coloured raspberries and have a tart-sweet, slightly floral and earthy flavour. A grocery store that stocks ingredients from Newfoundland may have them bottled or frozen. Otherwise, try European markets or Scandinavian specialty stores. If all you can find is a cloudberry or bakeapple preserve, add it to the simmering fruit but reduce the amount of sugar. Cloudberry liqueur is available at most liquor stores. If you can't find it, the recipe won't suffer if you omit it.

Nutritional Value Per Serving (234 g): Calories 402, Protein 5.4 g, Carbohydrates 42 g, Dietary Fibre 2.7 g, Sugars 23 g, Total Fat 25 g, Saturated Fat 15 g, Cholesterol 165 mg, Sodium 125 mg

Warm Banana Pecan Cake

Catch
RESTAURANT & OYSTER BAR

TOPPING:
(mix all the ingredients together)
½ cup (125 ml) brown sugar, lightly packed
½ cup (125 ml) English toffee pieces
½ cup (125 ml) chopped pecans
¼ cup (65 ml) sugar
2 tbsp (30 ml) cocoa
½ tsp (2 ml) cinnamon
Pinch nutmeg

CARAMEL SAUCE:
½ cup (125 ml) sugar
⅓ cup (85 ml) water
3 tbsp (45 ml) bourbon

3 tbsp (45 ml) butter
½ tsp (2 ml) vanilla paste
Juice of ¼ lemon
Pinch salt

CAKE:
1 cup (250 ml) butter, softened
1 cup (250 ml) sugar
3 very ripe bananas
8 eggs
¼ cup (65 ml) vegetable oil
2 cups (500 ml) flour
1 tsp (5 ml) cinnamon

½ tsp (2 ml) baking powder
½ cup (125 ml) milk chocolate chips
¼ cup (65 ml) English toffee pieces
¼ cup (65 ml) chopped pecans

BOURBON ICE CREAM:
½ cup (125 ml) sugar
9 egg yolks
2¾ cups (690 ml) 35% cream
¼ cup (65 ml) brown sugar, lightly packed
⅓ cup (85 ml) bourbon

CARAMEL SAUCE: Heat a saucepan on medium. Add a small amount of sugar and let caramelize to a golden-brown. Slowly add more sugar, allowing it to caramelize after each addition. Mix together remaining ingredients and very slowly add to the caramelized sugar. If using a gas stove, turn off heat. The caramelized sugar will harden in the pan, but this is normal. Turn heat to medium-low and stir occasionally. Once the caramelized sugar has dissolved, take off heat and set aside.

CAKE: Heat oven to 325°F (160°C). In a standing mixer with paddle attachment, cream the butter, sugar and bananas. Add eggs one at a time, then vegetable oil. Mix the dry ingredients and add to mixing bowl. Mix just until the batter comes together. Using a spatula, stir in the chocolate chips, toffee and pecans. Place a silicone dome mould on a baking sheet. Put 1 tbsp (15 ml) topping followed by 1 tbsp (15 ml) caramel sauce into each cavity (the remainder will be used to decorate the plates). Gently spoon in cake batter, taking care not to disturb the caramel sauce and topping. Bake until a toothpick inserted in the centre comes out clean, about 25 minutes. Let cool to room temperature. Place in the freezer for 24 hours. Remove from moulds and return to freezer.

BOURBON ICE CREAM: In a medium bowl, whisk the sugar and egg yolks. In a saucepan on medium heat, warm the cream, brown sugar and bourbon. When the mixture begins to simmer, slowly add it to the sugar-yolk mixture, whisking constantly. Pour back into the pan and continue cooking over medium heat until slightly thickened and coats the back of a spoon. Make sure it doesn't boil. Remove from heat. Strain into a large container and cool. Transfer to an ice cream maker and freeze according to the manufacturer's instructions.

TO ASSEMBLE: The day before serving, remove the desired quantity of cakes from the freezer and defrost, covered with plastic wrap, on a plate in your fridge. When ready to serve, warm in a 300°F (150°C) oven for 10 minutes. Sprinkle each plate with slices of banana. Drizzle with caramel sauce and top with an individual cake and a scoop of ice cream.

Makes 24 muffin-size cakes.

Nutritional Value Per Serving (127 g), Calories 431, Protein 5.4 g, Carbohydrates 38 g, Dietary Fibre 1.5 g, Sugars 26 g, Total Fat 29 g, Saturated Fat 14.7 g, Cholesterol 205 mg, Sodium 143 mg

Lobby on York: 01 executive chef Joe Dokuchie **02** chef Rolf Hagen **03** chef Lara Thordarson **Blue Water Cafe: 04** executive chef Frank Pabst **05** pastry chef Jean-Pierre Sanchez **Cafe Brio: 06** executive chef Laurie Munn **Fairmont Chateau Whistler: 07** executive chef Vincent Stufano **Garde Manger: 08** executive chef Chuck Hughes **La Buca: 09** executive chef Andrey Durbach **La Chronique: 10** executive chef Marc de Canck **Primo & Secondo: 11** executive chef Roberto Stabile **Wasabi: 12** executive chef Cho Venevongsa **13** executive chef William Wong **Araxi: 14** executive chef James Walt **15** pastry chef Aaron Heath **West: 16** executive chef Warren Geraghty **17** pastry chef Rhonda Viani **Mistura: 18** executive chef Massimo Capra **19** chef Derek Von Raesfeld **Bacalao: 20** executive chef Mike Barsky **21** pastry chef Andrea Maunder **Wellington Gastro Pub: 22** executive chef Chris Deraiche **Opus: 23** executive chef Jason Cox **Auberge du Pommier: 24** executive chef Jason Bangerter **25** sous chef John Horne **La Montée: 26** executive chef Martin Juneau **CinCin: 27** executive chef Francois Gagnon **28** pastry chef Thierry Busset **Scaramouche: 29** executive chef Keith Frogett **Nota Bene: 30** executive chef David Lee **River Café: 31** executive chef Scott Pohorelic **The Only On King: 32** executive chef Jason Schubert **33** executive chef Paul Harding **Fairmont Waterfront: 34** executive chef Patrick Doré **Da Maurizio: 35** executive chef Andrew King **Catch: 36** executive chef Hayato Okamitsu **37** pastry chef Allison Okamitsu **Fairmont Royal York: 38** executive chef Ryan Gustafson **Chiado: 39** executive chef Manuel Vilela **Taverne sur le Square: 40** executive chef Stephen Leslie

The Recipes by Restaurant

Toronto

Auberge du Pommier 4150 Yonge St., Toronto, Ontario 416 222 2220
Œuf Poché with Asparagus and Pickled Mushrooms	17
Salade Auberge du Pommier	59
Poussin Rôti with Braised Savoy Cabbage and Apple-Juniper Broth	117
Seared Tuna with Ragoût de Légumes aux Épices Marocains	163
Pain Perdu with Strawberry-Rhubarb Purée	177

Chiado 864 College St., Toronto, Ontario 416 538 1910
Risotto of Lobster	79
Pheasant	109
Natas do Ceu Cream of Heaven	173

Fairmont
Spring Lamb Ravioli with Morels and Fava Beans (Vancouver) 900 West Georgia St., Vancouver, British Columbia 604 684 3131	91
East Coast Scallops (Royal York) 100 Front St. West, Toronto, Ontario 866 840 8402	160
Maple Syrup-Glazed Cedar Roast Salmon with Fingerling Potatoes and Red Onion Marmalade (Whistler) 4599 Chateau Blvd., Whistler, British Columbia 604 938 8000	164

Mistura 265 Davenport Rd., Toronto, Ontario 416 515 0009
Acquacotta The Stone Soup of Italy	36
Asparagus Cannelloni	80
Glazed Veal Brisket with Chestnut, Cipolline and Squash Sauté	113
Balsamico-Glazed Lamb Ribs	114
Chocolate Salame with Zabaglione Sauce	174

Nota Bene 180 Queen St. West, Toronto, Ontario 416 977 6400
Yucatan Hot and Sour Soup	39
Grilled Calamari Salad	56
Seared Rare Bigeye Tuna with Green Papaya Salad	147

Opus 37 Prince Arthur Ave., Toronto, Ontario 416 921 3105
Shrimp with Fennel and Apple Salad	2
Mixed Organic Greens, Vegetable Chips and a Champagne Vinaigrette	55
Cornish Hen with Root Vegetables, Parmesan Gnocchi and Savoury Jus	110
Red Snapper and Green Bean Salad in Chive Jus	143

Scaramouche 1 Benvenuto Place, Toronto, Ontario 416 961 8011
Beef Carpaccio with Raw Asparagus, Blood Orange, Fennel and Endive Lettuces	5
Mussel and Saffron Soup	35
Arctic Char in Tomato Water with a Fine Herb Mayonnaise	144

Montreal

La Chronique 99 Laurier West , Montreal, Quebec 514 271 3095
Shrimp Salad with Shiitake Mushrooms, Basil and Vermicelli Noodles	68
Duck Confit Risotto with Seared Foie Gras	95
Butternut Squash Gnocchi	96
Duck Breast with Maple Syrup and Rose Petals	129

Garde Manger 408 Saint-François-Xavier, Montreal, Quebec 514 678 5044
Lentil and Goat Cheese Bruschetta	22
Tomato, Avocado and Ricotta Salata	71
Braised Short Ribs on Garlic Mashed Potatoes with Fiddleheads and Yellow Beets	130
Seafood Platter	167

La Montée 1424 Bishop, Montreal, Quebec 514 289 9921
Braised Bacon Burgundy-Style with Marinated Mushrooms and Onions and Red Wine Jelly	21
Piglet's Belly Confit with Grilled Peppers and Fresh Cream	125
White Chocolate and Vanilla Cream with Oranges	190

Primo & Secondo 7023 St-Dominique, Montreal, Quebec 514 908 0838
Risi e Bisi	87
Tagliatelle con Rapini, Saisiccia e Pomodori Cilegi	103
Trippa Calda alla Parmigiana/ Trippe with melted parmesan	121
Tiramisu	189

Taverne sur le Square 1 Westmount Square, Montreal, Quebec 514 989 9779
Salmon Tartare with Southwest Spices	13
Grilled Calamari Salad	64
Quebec Rack of Lamb with Warm Radicchio, Fennel and Pine Nut Salad	122

Halifax

Da Maurizio 1496 Lower Water, Halifax, Nova Scotia 902 423 0859
Polenta con Funghi e Gorgonzola	29
Minestrone al Pesto	48
Fettucine all'Aragosta	99
Saltimbocca alla Romana	138

St. John's

Bacalao 65 Lemarchant Rd., St. John's, Newfoundland 709 579 6565
Salade Niçoise à la Bacalao	75
Bacalao à la Russe	104
Moose Tourtière with Partridgeberry Mustard	137
Bakeapple Cream Puffs	193

The making of the book

It's your health

Presented by the registered dietitians
at Dairy Farmers of Canada
www.dairygoodness.ca

100% CANADIAN MILK

Nourish the Healthy Eating Habit

You are your children's most influential role model. If you make healthy eating based on the Four Food Groups a family affair—you'll all benefit.

GETTING WHAT YOU'RE MISSING

Try cooking at home more often. It's much easier to have balanced four-food-group meals that everyone likes.

Replace soft drinks and fruit drinks with milk or chocolate milk, and warm up with hot chocolate or a latte.

Eat cheese on whole-grain toast in the morning, have yogourt and fruit for dessert and snacks.

Think milk-based vegetable soups and salads with extra veggies and cheese.

EYE-OPENING SURVEY

The most recent *Canadian Community Health Survey* showed that while some children don't consume enough milk products, by age 10 to 16, 61% of boys and a shocking 83% of girls don't meet even their recommended *minimum* three daily servings. How come? While there are many reasons for this situation, one of them is likely the eating habits of their most important role models—their parents.

FOOD GROUP ALERT

The same survey showed milk products to be the most underconsumed food group among adults of all ages, followed by vegetables and fruit. This means that a large majority of adults consume less than two servings of milk products a day and also miss out on fruits and vegetables. Other studies show that children whose mothers and fathers eat well and exercise regularly are more likely to have healthy lifestyles. Get the picture?

SIMPLY IRREPLACEABLE

Milk is our most reliable source of calcium and a source of 15 other essential nutrients. Cultivate a taste for milk and you'll be nourishing a habit with lifelong benefits.

For example an 8 oz/250 ml glass of milk provides the following % of our daily needs:

Calcium	28%
Vitamin D	45%
Vitamin B_{12}	57%
Riboflavin	30%
Phosphorus	22%

TRI-COLOUR PENNE

This is so good and so quick to make, you'll be amazed! Serves 4.

3⅔ cups	penne	900 ml
2 tbsp	flour	30 ml
2 cups	milk	500 ml
⅓ cup	basil pesto or more to taste	80 ml
2 cups	cooked chopped broccoli	500 ml
2 cups	cherry tomatoes, halved	500 ml
4 tbsp	grated Parmesan cheese	60 ml

In large pot of boiling salted water, cook pasta for 10 min or until almost tender. Drain and return to pot. Whisk flour into milk and pour over pasta. Stir in pesto. Cook over medium heat, stirring, until sauce thickens, about 3-5 minutes. Gently add broccoli. Reheat about 1 minute. Season with salt and pepper. Stir in tomato halves and serve, sprinkled with the Parmesan.

Tasteful!

The simple elegance of your meal
presentation is surpassed only
by the sumptuous flavours enhanced
by the features unique to our
enamelled cast iron cookware.

Add your name to the global list of
distinguished chefs and fine restaurants
that have chosen to
taste the Staub difference.

staub
en France

The Fairmont Waterfront, Vancouver

Fairmont
HOTELS & RESORTS

PROUD TO SUPPORT CANADA
COOKS FOR AUTISM RESEARCH

Take a vacation from the ordinary

Discover Canada the Fairmont way. Our long history of luxurious, graceful
hospitality and landmark hotels is a perfect match for the style and romance
of some of North America's finest destinations—whether in Toronto at
The Fairmont Royal York, Vancouver at The Fairmont Waterfront or in the
mountains at The Fairmont Chateau Whistler.

Enjoy fabulous locally-sourced cuisine and award-winning Canadian wines,
accented with some of the warmest service you'll ever experience. Whichever
destination you choose, a visit to Fairmont Hotels & Resorts will leave you
revived and exhilarated.

For reservations or more information, please contact your travel professional,
call 1 800 441 1414 or visit www.fairmont.com

  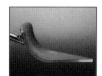

Van Houtte

—

is proud to be

—

"Cooking with Canada's Best"

—

in support of

—

The Kilee Patchell-Evans

—

Autism Research Group

Master Roaster of Fine Coffees Since 1919

Building a better community starts with the right foundation.

Creating a vital, healthy community is a group effort. And at the heart of it, you'll find local organizations, fuelled by committed people who are passionate about building a better future for us all. That's why RBC® celebrates community-based organizations through the contribution of our resources, time and talents. Together we can build the right foundation for our community.

To find out more, go to **www.rbc.com/responsibility**.

We are proud to support the **Kilee Patchell-Evans Autism Research Group**.

CREATE
A BETTER FUTURE

® Registered trademark of Royal Bank of Canada.